# MACRAMÉ
# COUTURE

# MACRAMÉ
# COUTURE

17 embellishment projects

Gwenaël Petiot

SCHIFFER
PUBLISHING

4880 Lower Valley Road  •  Atglen, PA 19310

Other Schiffer Books on Related Subjects:

*Artisan Felting: Wearable Art*, Jenny Hill,
ISBN 978-0-7643-5852-4

*Macrame Fashion Accessories & Jewelry*, Sylvie Hooghe,
ISBN 978-0-7643-4857-0

*The Dharma of Fashion*, Otto von Busch,
ISBN 978-0-7643-5894-4

Library of Congress Control Number: 2020933407

"Schiffer," "Schiffer Publishing, Ltd.," and the pen and inkwell
logo are registered trademarks of Schiffer Publishing, Ltd.
Produced by BlueRed Press Ltd. 2019
Designed by Insight Design Concepts Ltd.
Type set in Neutra Text

ISBN: 978-0-7643-5991-0
Printed in Malaysia

Published by Schiffer Publishing, Ltd.
4880 Lower Valley Road
Atglen, PA 19310
Phone: (610) 593-1777; Fax: (610) 593-2002
Email: Info@schifferbooks.com
Web: www.schifferbooks.com

For our complete selection of fine books on this and related
subjects, please visit our website at www.schifferbooks.com.
You may also write for a free catalog.

Schiffer Publishing's titles are available at special discounts
for bulk purchases for sales promotions or premiums. Special
editions, including personalized covers, corporate imprints, and
excerpts, can be created in large quantities for special needs.
For more information, contact the publisher.

We are always looking for people to write books on new and
related subjects. If you have an idea for a book, please contact
us at proposals@schifferbooks.com.

A huge thanks to Jo Bryant, Virginie Pérocheau, Mélanie
Devisme, and Zineb Bensada.

# Contents

Introduction     6

Materials     8

Knots     14

Beginner Projects     26

    Wide-Collar Jacket     28

    Jacket Front-Pocket Strip     34

    Fringe Necklace     38

    Headband     42

    Flip-Flops     46

Intermediate Projects     50

    Wide Cuff     52

    Long Jacket Strip     56

    Sandal Anklets     62

    Belt     68

    Banana Bag Strap     72

    Fringed Choker Necklace     78

    Yoga Shirt Backstrap     82

Advanced Projects     88

    Macramé Tiara     90

    Flower Barrette     98

    Clutch Bag     106

    Mandala Bag     112

    Tribal Drawing Denim Jacket Back     118

# INTRODUCTION

Macramé is the ancient craft of hand-knotting string or yarn to create intricate textile decorations and patterns. As with many crafts, macramé has gone in and out of favor, but it's currently very fashionable. Its previous heyday was in the 1960s and 1970s during the hippie movement, when bohemian creations such as wall and plant hangings were all the rage—before that, macramé had last been popular during Victorian times.

Now the technique has enjoyed a rebirth over the last decade or so, thanks in part to new knot combinations and different kinds of source materials and textiles, as well as the general renewed interest in all kinds of crafting. Exciting young designers have embraced macramé and extended its use into previously unexplored areas such as high fashion and decorative jewelry.

Personally, after learning macramé techniques from local artists during my travels in South America, I was given the rare opportunity by a celebrated French clothes designer to work with her during Paris Fashion Week. She wanted me to collaborate and add my macramé creations to her couture outfits. This amazing offer opened an entire world of macramé possibilities for me—I got to customize numerous items such as jackets, handbags, hats, and even shoes—and this really opened my eyes as to what can be done with this wonderful craft.

I have poured much of my knowledge into this book, so that you will be able to achieve a variety of different projects for your own outfits. To keep things simple, I have used only five easy knots, but arranged in different ways and with varying color combinations you can customize your own clothes and make totally unique accessories. My tutorials are suitable for beginners as well as advanced knotters, and with practice, you will be able to create them all and even have the knowledge to create your own designs and ideas. But remember that, as with any skill, patience is the absolute key to success.

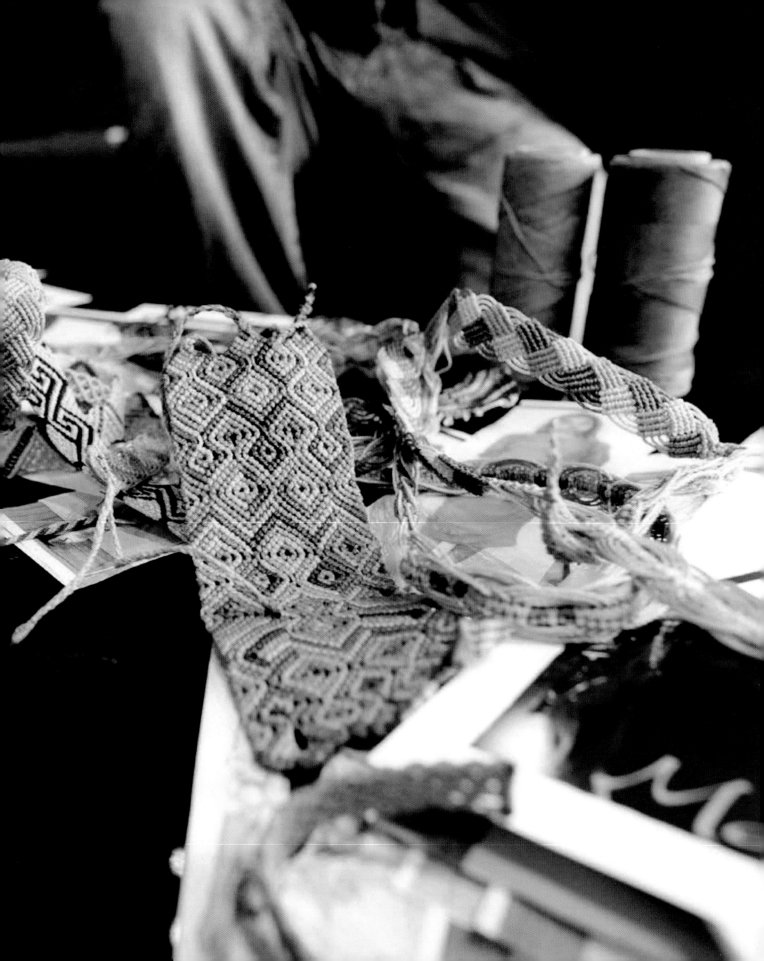

# MATERIALS

Macramé requires very few tools. This is a list of the basic supplies you will need to follow the step-by-step projects:

### HOLDING BOARD AND CLIPS

You will need one holding board, plus at least two large clips. These are necessary to secure your threads as you work on the knotting, and will hold your knots correctly and securely. You can use any kind of rigid board (wood or plastic) but to facilitate weaving it needs to be at least 8 x 12 in. (20 x 30 cm).

For most of the projects you will need a holding board thread that you will clip horizontally across your board. This thread is used to install (i.e., hold on to) your thread strands before starting weaving. The thread has to be as long as the board is wide, but in most cases, its color does not matter since it will be pulled off and discarded once the knotting is done.

### MACRAMÉ THREADS

Macramé can be knotted with any kind of cord or threads, including wool, hemp, silk, jute, or even leather, as well as a variety of synthetic cords. In this book I mainly use 1 mm thick waxed polyester threads for the different projects. I really like to use this material because on completion of a creation it can be melted after cutting the cord ends. It gives a great stiff, neat finish to pieces. It's waterproof, flexible, and very strong at the same time. There are many colors and it's very reasonably priced. I also use 2–3 mm unwaxed polyester and cotton cords for some step-by-step projects. This type of fiber gives a nice bohemian touch to macramé work. However, if you want to, you can choose your own threads to do these projects, but keep in mind that they must be the same width to re create the same project at the same size.

## SEWING THREADS AND NEEDLE

These are used when you need to sew your macramé pieces onto your clothing, but they are also used to join two or more macramé knottings together (as is necessary with a number of my projects) or to add sew-on snap fasteners to fabric. The color of the sewing threads used for each project is an important consideration. If you want it to be invisible, it must be the same color as the macramé thread around which you stitch your sewing. When I have to join two different-colored macramé pieces together, or simply if I don't have the right thread color, I use transparent nylon thread, such as fishing line, to be certain that the seams are not visible.

## RULER AND SCISSORS

A ruler is useful for measuring the strings/threads before starting a project. When you need to cut long-length threads, a measuring tape is essential to make things easier. Small scissors with good sharp, fine tips are necessary to cut the thread cleanly. Blunt scissors damage and fray threads and leave ends that will spoil the look of your piece.

# LIGHTER AND TEXTILE GLUE

Synthetic threads need to be cauterized after you cut them at the end of each project so that the last knots do not loosen and untie themselves. Thread burners are especially made for this kind of handicraft, but an ordinary lighter is good enough, or even a simple candle flame (though this isn't as easy to handle). When you finish a project, numerous thread ends will be sticking out of the knotting. Cut these remains to leave just a couple of millimeters and—very carefully—burn or melt the extremity for a couple of seconds, then lightly press on it to fix the weld, waiting a few seconds so you don't burn yourself.

Natural threads such as cotton will not melt; instead you have to use a textile glue to secure the knots. Cut the thread close to the last knot, leaving just sufficient length on which you put a small drop of glue to secure its end. Glue can also be useful when you need to attach a macramé weaving onto a piece of clothing.

# SEW-ON SNAP FASTENERS

These small fastening devices made of metal or plastic are generally used instead of buttons. The snap is worked by pressing its two round halves together, one pushed into the other. Unlike common snap fasteners that need a special tool to install, these sew-on snaps—the ones with two or four small holes—can easily be added by using a couple of hitch knots with your sewing needle and thread.

## Attaching the Macramé

These instructions cover the basics of hand-sewing your macramé embellishment pieces together or onto clothing, etc. Sewing is usually necessary to join two (or more) pieces of macramé together, to directly attach your weaving onto your clothes, or to add snaps.

Cut a strand of thread to the length you need—or twice the length if you are doubling the thread. Then thread a sturdy needle. There are two ways to do this: with a single or with doubled thread. I prefer to use the latter, so that's the one I will explain—but you can choose either way. Pass your thread through the needle hole—you can use a needle threader if you struggle with this—then pull the end of the thread until the lengths are even. This gives you two tail ends. To secure the thread, make a knot using both ends. Join both ends together and wrap them about three times around your middle finger. Keep the thread end(s) between your thumb and middle finger and roll the ends between both fingers before passing them inside the loop as if you were doing a simple overhand knot. Pull on both ends to create the knot.

When joining two macramé pieces together of the same color, use a sewing thread with the same color. But if the weavings have different colors, it's often better to use a transparent nylon thread, such as fine fishing line, so your stitches will not be visible from the front. After threading your needle, place both macramé weavings together at the angle you want to sew them, and pass your needle in and out from the underneath/backside up and through between two knots of the first row. Be sure the knot you made to secure your doubled thread is big enough to stay securely between the macramé knots. Then insert your needle from front to back inside the second piece. Repeat, by pushing the needle back to the front but two rows farther along. Keep repeating this until the full length of the seam is complete. To secure your last stitch so that the thread does not come out, simply make a loop under the weaving into the last stitch you made, and then draw the needle through it. When you pull on it tightly, you will make a knot that secures the stitch.

---

**ADVICE**

I strongly suggest that you carefully read each of the step-by-step sections before starting the step itself, so as to completely understand what you are doing at each stage. Taken bit by bit, and broken down into pieces, even complicated instructions become much easier.

# KNOTS

## HOLDING THREAD/CORD

This section will help you learn about different knots and macramé techniques. To understand macramé knots, you need to comprehend the crucial difference between the holding thread and the knotting thread or cord.

The holding thread is the foundation of the entire work and is the line that the knot is tied around—it is sometimes called the knot bearer. It gives the direction of your work, and it's important that it holds firm and steady while you are making a knot. When the knotting is complete, the holding thread is usually completely hidden inside the macramé.

## KNOTTING CORD

The knotting thread is the moving thread and is simply the one you use to actually make the knot. It is part of the project itself.

However, the holding and knotting threads can change positions as the pattern progresses; a cord that is the holding thread in one step can become the knotting cord in another step. It may look confusing, but don't worry—practice all the basic knots several times until you can make regular, neat knots. Knowing each knot perfectly will make things a lot easier when you start your step-by-step projects!

## OVERHAND KNOT

The overhand knot is the simplest type of knot that people use every day. For macramé it's usually used to install the strands before weaving them, to add a color row in the pattern, or to secure a bead or the end of a strand to keep the ends from fraying. You can tie this knot by crossing the thread ends—usually around a holding cord—to form a loop (step 1) and bringing one end through the loop before pulling on both ends (step 2).

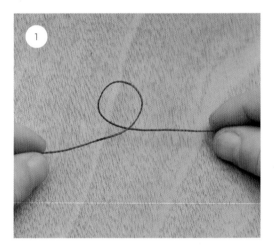

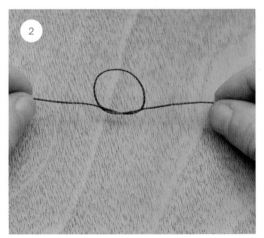

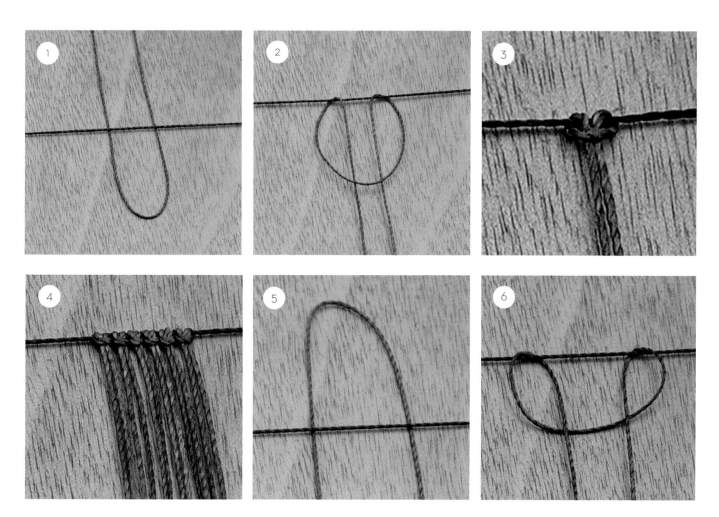

## LARK'S HEAD KNOT
## (AND REVERSE LARK'S HEAD KNOT)

As with the overhand knot, the lark's head knot is used mostly for the mounting stages before weaving, but it can also be used to add a new color in the pattern. To practice it, secure a holding thread horizontally to your board and fold in half the thread you want to tie. Place it under the holding strand, the folded part at the bottom and both ends at the top (step 1). Bring the two ends over the holding cord and pass them under the folding loop (step 2) before pulling both ends together to tie the knot (steps 3 and 4).

A reverse lark's head knot is made by passing the knotting thread under the holding thread, with both ends facing you (step 5), bringing the loop above the holding cord and passing the ends over the loop before pulling them tight (step 6).

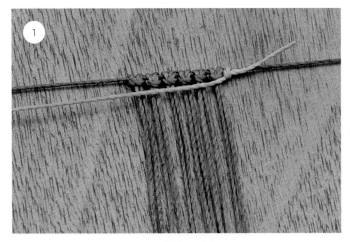

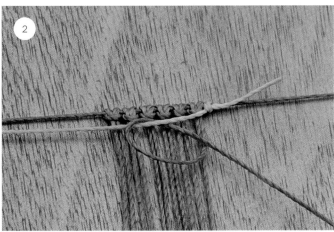

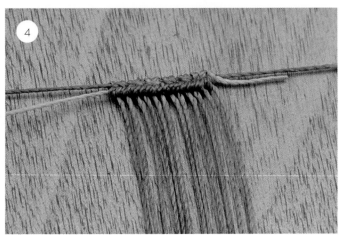

### Horizontal and Diagonal double half hitch knot

The double half hitch knot is the knot you will use the most to create the projects in this book. It can be made horizontally, diagonally, and vertically, but also from right to left or from left to right. All directions need to be practiced so they can be easily made when needed. In the step-by-step projects, when I use the term "line"

this is the kind of knot you have to use. Here I use a light green cord for the holding cord and blue for the knotting ones. To make a horizontal line from right to left, firmly pull the holding cord with your left hand in the opposite direction (step 1), while with the right hand, loop the next cord, passing it under, then over, the holding cord, then finally inside the loop above itself (step 2). Pull on it and

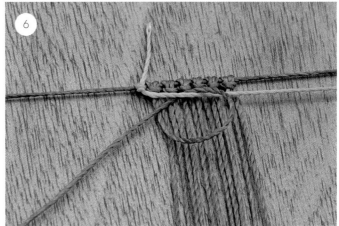

your single half hitch knot is done. Make a second similar loop with the same cord to complete your double half hitch knot (step 3). By tying a series of knots with several knotting threads, a line shape will form (step 4). To make a line from left to right, use your right hand to tension the holding cord (step 5), and with your left hand make the loops exactly in the same way (steps 6, 7, and 8).

The diagonal double half hitch knot is tied exactly the same way as the horizontal one, except that the holding strand is held at a diagonal. You will need to adjust the tension while making your knots so that your line keeps working in the direction you want.

## VERTICAL DOUBLE HALF HITCH KNOT

As opposed to the horizontal double half hitch knot, the vertical knot uses only one knotting cord to tie the knots and several holding cords. Here I have shown the knotting cord in blue and the holding cords in light green. In the step-by-step projects, when I use the term "row," this is the kind of knot you have to use.

To do a vertical knot, make a loop using just the knotting cord, passing it under, then over, the holding thread and then inside the loop above it (step 1). Do this twice to complete the knot (step 2). Before tying the second half, be sure the first loop is tightly placed against the previous knot. The vertical double knot is repeated each time, using the next cord as the holding thread until the end of the row (steps 3 and 4). The images below show the row working from left to right; the images on page 21 show the row working from right to left (steps 5, 6, 7, and 8).

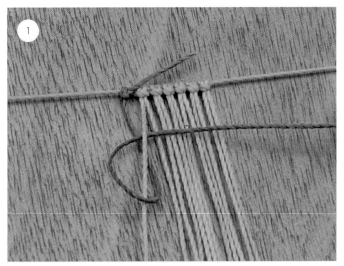

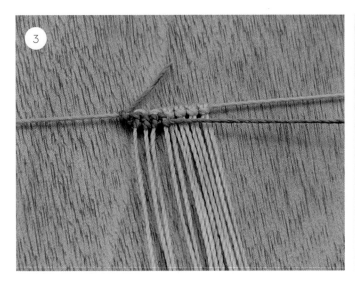

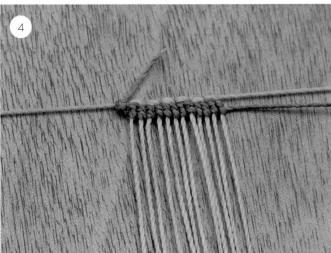

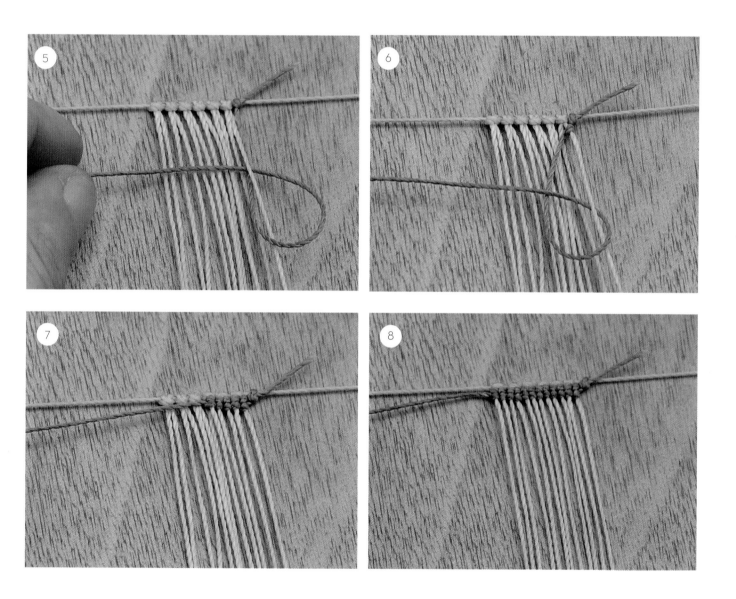

## SQUARE KNOT OR FLAT KNOT

Fix three strands with simple overhand knots on a clipped holding board. Both outer brown cords are the knotting cords, and the central orange strand is the holding thread (step 1), which means this strand will be inside the knot and won't be visible once the square knot is tied. In some projects you will be instructed to do this knot with two or three holding cords, but the way to do this is exactly the same.

Move the left knotting thread over the holding cord to create a loop, under the right cord (step 2). Then the right cord goes under the holding thread and comes up in the loop over the left thread (step 3). Pull on both ends to tie the knot (step 4). The first half of the knot is done: this is a half square knot. To complete it, repeat the first steps, BUT this time use the right strand to make the first

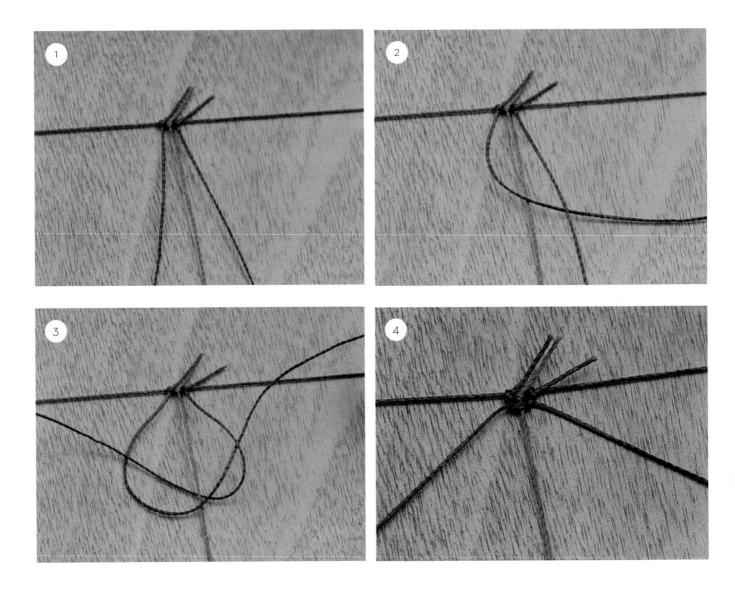

loop, moving it over the holding thread, then under the left knotting thread (step 5). Now pass the left thread under the holding cord and bring it up in the loop (step 6). Pull on both ends to complete the full flat square knot (step 7). Repeated square knots create a flat braid pattern (step 8). To make a neat knot, the holding thread needs to have tension, so fix it tightly with a clip at the bottom of your board or hold it between your teeth while the knot is tied!

## SPIRAL SQUARE KNOT

If half square knots are repeated over and over—meaning that the first loop on the same side is used every time a knot is made—a spiral pattern will emerge. It makes no difference whether this is started on the right or left side.

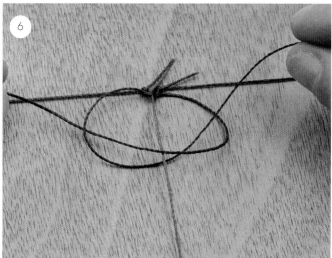

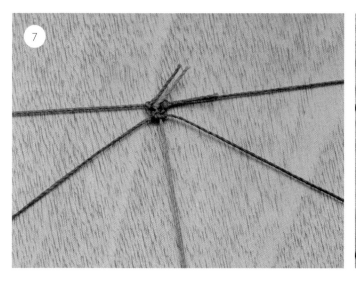

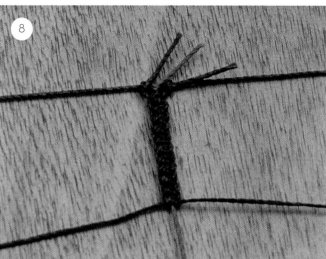

## THREE-STRAND BRAID

This is the commonest braid or plait. To practice it, install three strands with simple overhand knots on a holding board thread already secured with clips. Bring the left strand over the center strand (step 1), then the right strand over the center strand (step 2). Keep moving the outer cords into the center (steps 3 and 4), holding the threads under tension as the plait progresses.

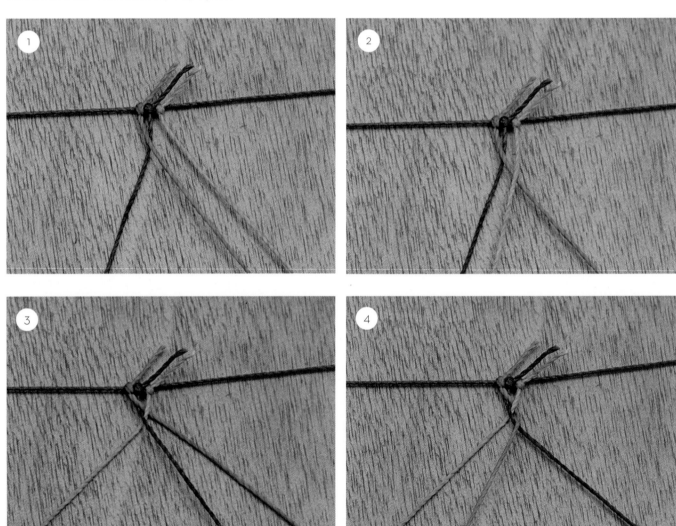

Once your braid has reached the desired length, secure it by making a tight overhand knot, using all three cords at the same time (step 5). To finish, cut the braid (step 6) above the knot and melt the ends if you use synthetic cords, or glue them if you use natural cords such as cotton.

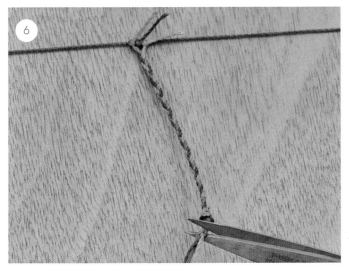

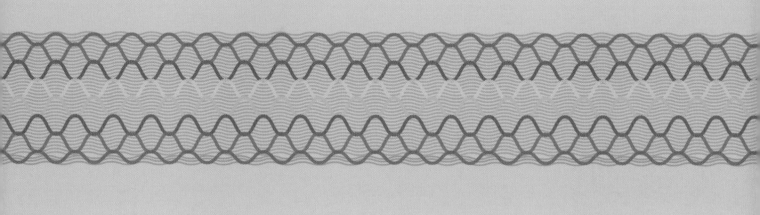

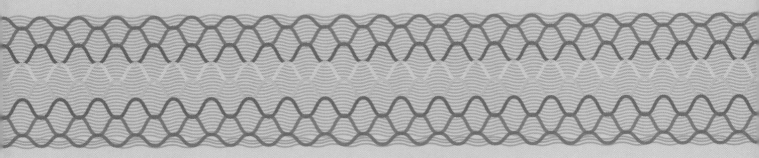

# BEGINNER PROJECTS

# WIDE-COLLAR JACKET

I originally made this wide-collar macramé for a fashion show, and it looked fantastic! Make one for yourself to transform a classy collarless jacket into a unique piece. Use similar shades to keep the look sophisticated, or knot your own creative piece by using totally different colors.

**Knots used:**

Diagonal double half hitch knot, overhand knot

**Macramé strands:**

All lengths of 1 mm waxed thread

8 x Light brown, 73 in. (185 cm)

16 x Dark navy blue, 73 in. (185 cm)

8 x Light navy blue, 73 in. (185 cm)

1 holding board strand, the width of the board

**Materials:**

One collarless jacket

Knotting board and clips

Needle and dark blue sewing thread/cord

Ruler and lighter

Scissors

**Dimensions:**

The width of the collar is about 2 in. (5 cm), depending on how tightly you tie your knots. The strand length given here is to create a 24 in. (60 cm) collar, but you can adjust this as you want: you need around 12 in. (30 cm) of threads to knot 4 in. (10 cm) of macramé weaving.

**STEP 1** Clip the holding cord horizontally across the board; its color does not matter since it is pulled off once the knotting is finished. Install the eight brown threads, using simple overhand knots but leaving the cords as short as possible above the holding cord, since these will be cut off later. Then place on each side eight dark navy blue and four light navy blue threads. From now on, only diagonal double half hitch knots are used.

**STEP 2** Knot both central cords together. Use these two same threads as holding cords and make one small diagonal line on each side with the next four threads. Keep using the same holding cords, and knot back the same knotting threads in the opposite direction. Join both holding cords together in the middle to create a diamond shape. (1, 2, 3, 4)

**STEP 3** Make another double half hitch knot with the same two cords, but work in the opposite direction. Keep using these same two cords as holding cords to knot the three threads on either side. (5, 6)

**STEP 4** Now you should have one blue strand left on each side of the diamond shape. Use them as holding cords to make one diagonal line on each side, using the next four threads attached on the holding board strand. (7)

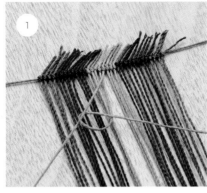

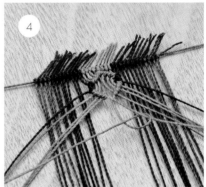

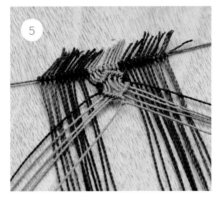

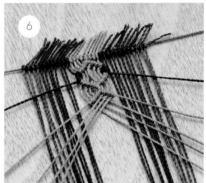

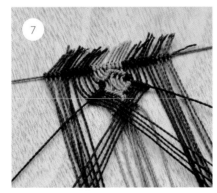

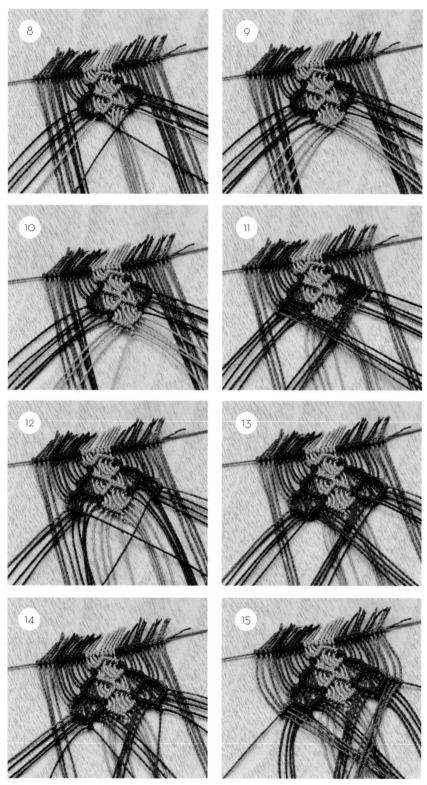

**STEP 5** Keep using the same holding cords to create a diamond shape on each side (as you did in step 2). When you join both cords to close the diamond shape, be sure to make the last knot perpendicular to the lines you just did. Make another diamond shape at the bottom to get four diamonds. Finally, make one last double half hitch knot at the base (exactly as before in step 3). (8, 9, 10)

**STEP 6** Use the farthest right and left knotted cords to make another line on each side, with the four next strands attached to the holding board cord. Then make both lines come back with the same knotting cords. Continue by closing the diamond shapes, making one more line on each side by using the central blue strands as holding cords. Make a last knot below the diamond shapes (as before in step 3). (11, 12, 13, 14)

**STEP 7** Repeat step 6 to add one more diamond shape on each side, but this time use just the three last cords (instead of four). Finally, complete both central diamonds. (15, 16, 17, 18)

**STEP 8** Repeat the previous steps as many times as you need to get the correct length for your macramé strip. Try doing this visually, using the diamond shapes as your guide. Don't worry if you have some difficulty doing the first shaped lines; it will get easier as you get the rhythm of the pattern in your head, and also because your strands will get shorter and easier to knot as you progress. (19, 20, 21)

**STEP 9** You now have to do a bit of calculating about when to stop your weaving to get the right size. The tip of the collar (created in the first steps) is about 1.3 in. (3 cm). This will be repeated at the other end, so to get the collar symmetrical you have to subtract about 2.5 in. (6 cm) from your total collar length, to know when to stop weaving. More precisely, if you want a 16 in. (40 cm) total length, you have to stop weaving at around 13.5 in. (34 cm) for the widest part of the collar (beginning tip is not included). (22)

**STEP 10** Time to knot the tip shape you knotted at the beginning, but this time upside down. Luckily it's easy. Leave the three farthest right and left cords. Complete the central diamond shape, plus one diamond on either side to get three of them. Leave four more strands on each side, then knot two diamond shapes below the central one. Complete the tip, leaving four more strands on each side, and knot a final central diamond. (23, 24, 25)

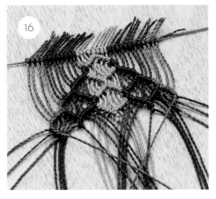
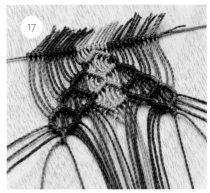
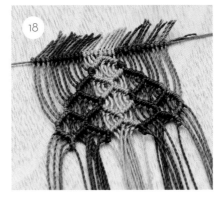
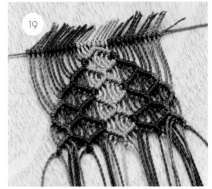
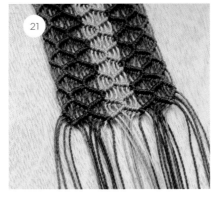
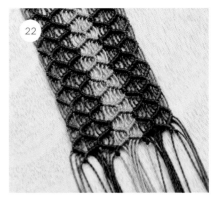
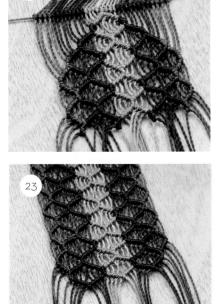
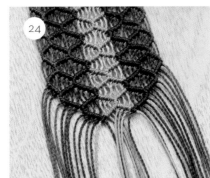
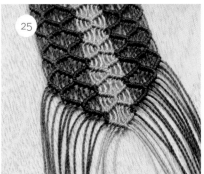

**STEP 11** Pull off the holding board cord. Cut the remains of the strands on each side and neatly burn the extremities to give a nice smooth finish.

**Attaching your Macramé**

For this project, finely stitch, using a matching color thread, your macramé to the jacket. (26)

# JACKET FRONT-POCKET STRIP

This small but colorful macramé strip will give a fun flourish and finishing touch to your classic denim jacket—making it particularly special and uniquely your own.

**Knots used:**

Diagonal double half hitch knot, lark's head knot, overhand knot

**Macramé strands:**

All lengths of 1 mm waxed thread

1 x Bright green, 102 in. (260 cm)

2 x White, 55 in. (140 cm)

2 x Blue, 55 in. (140 cm)

2 x Yellow, 55 in. (140 cm)

6 x Fuchsia pink, 55 in. (140 cm)

1 holding board strand, the width of the board

**Materials:**

One denim jacket with front pocket

Knotting board and clips

Needle and white sewing cord

Ruler and lighter

Scissors

Textile glue (optional)

**Dimensions:**

The width of the strip is about 1 in. (2.5 cm), depending on how tightly you tie your knots. The strand length given here is to make a 14 in. (35 cm) macramé strip, but you can easily make it longer, knowing that you will need about 16 in. (40 cm) of cords (x 2 for the center one) to make an extra 4 in. (10 cm) of weaving.

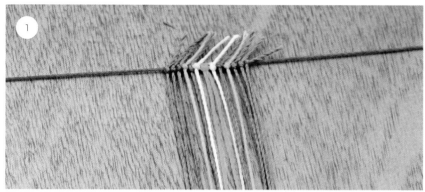

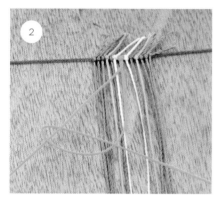

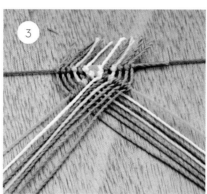

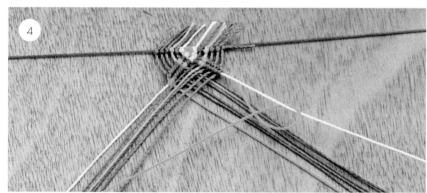

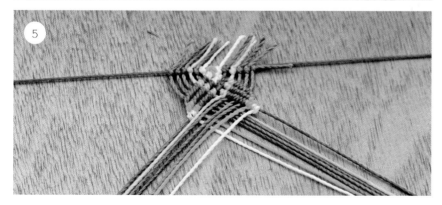

**STEP 1** Using the clips, install the holding board cord horizontally across the board—the color doesn't matter since it is pulled off at the end. Fold in half the bright green strand and knot it with a lark's head knot. Place one white strand on either side, using a simple overhand knot, then do the same with the blue ones and then the yellow ones, and finally add three pink threads on each side. (1)

**STEP 2** From now on, only diagonal double half hitch knots will be used. Knot both green strands together with a double half hitch knot and use these two same threads as holding cords to make two diagonal lines going out from the middle to both sides. (2,3)

**STEP 3** Repeat step 2 to create a second line by knotting both central white threads together, then using them as holding cords. When you get to the end of these lines, you also have to tie the green cords coming out from the first ones. (4)

**STEP 4** Repeat step 3, using the blue threads as the holding cords. Do not forget to knot them together first, and also to tie the white threads at the end of these third lines. (5)

**STEP 5** Now the aim is to make a line on both sides, running from the sides to the center. For this, keep using the blue threads as holding cords and knot back across the same cords but in the reverse order—your holding cords have to be held at the same angle, and your knotting threads have to be firmly tied to create a kind of diamond shape. When you have completed one line on each side, tie both blue cords together to join them. (6)

**STEP 6** Repeat the previous step twice more to create two more lines. The first time, use the white cords as holding cords; the second time, use the green ones. Do not forget to tie the holding cords when they meet in the middle. (7, 8)

**STEP 7** Keep repeating from step 2 through to step 6 until the size of your macramé strip is the right length to fit your jacket. It must be finished with three lines going from the sides back to the center. (9, 10)

**STEP 8** Unclip your holding board cord and pull it off before cutting and neatly melting every outstanding thread. (11)

**Attaching your Macramé**

Now you need to attach the strip to your jacket. Open the front pocket and carefully pass the button through the first diamond shape. With your needle and thread, sew a knot on each white side of the strip until you near the lower part of your jacket. Instead of sewing, you could use a textile glue. (12, 13)

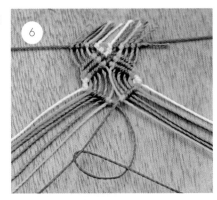
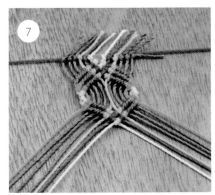
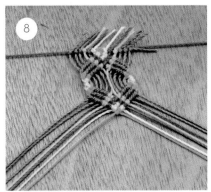
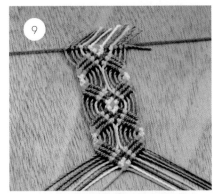

# FRINGE NECKLACE

This simple but fashionable white fringe necklace will enhance any summer outfit whether smart or casual. Wear it when you want to be noticed!

**Knots used:**

Flat square knot, reverse lark's head knot

**Macramé strands:**

All lengths of 2 mm white nylon

1 x 16 in. (40 cm)

42 x 91 in. (230 cm)

**Materials:**

Cord crimp clasps (to pinch or to glue)

Knotting board and clips

Pliers or glue

Scissors

Ruler and lighter

**Dimensions:**

These instructions will give you a 45 in. (115 cm) long, hanging fringe necklace. To know how long to cut the 42 threads—you can make it shorter or longer—multiply its final length by 2. The length of the neck cord is adjustable in the penultimate step.

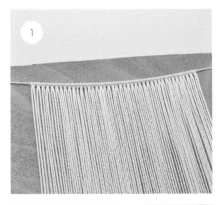

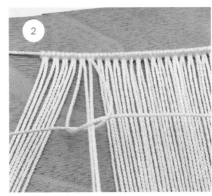

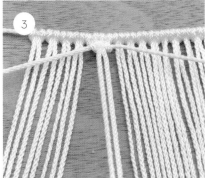

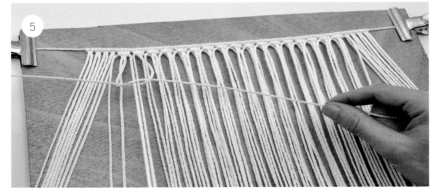

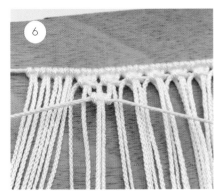

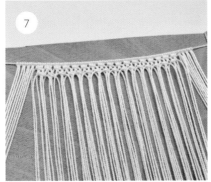

**STEP 1** Turn your board to work across the width, and securely clip the 16 in. (40 cm) strand. Install all the threads making reverse lark's head knots, but taking care that they are folded exactly in the middle and well centered on the clipped thread. (1)

**STEP 2** Start with the left-side cords. Leave the eight first strands alone—these won't be woven at all—and with the next four cords make a flat square knot with two threads inside the knot. Each knot has to be knotted tightly up against the preceding knot. (2, 3)

**STEP 3** Work on the right-hand side and repeat step 2 sixteen times. Work with four strands at a time. Do not knot the last eight farthest-right strands. (4)

**STEP 4** Return to the left side to work with both first square knots. Leave the two farthest-left cords of your first square knot and the two farthest-right cords of your second square knot. With the four remaining strands, make a square knot leaving a small 0.4 in. (1 cm) cord gap below the previous knots. Make another similar knot between the second and third square knot and repeat this 14 more times until you reach the farthest-right square knot. Leave untouched the two farthest-right strands. (5, 6, 7)

8

9

10

11

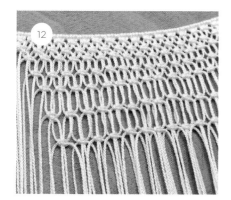

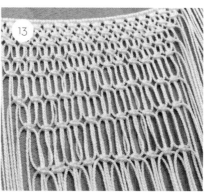

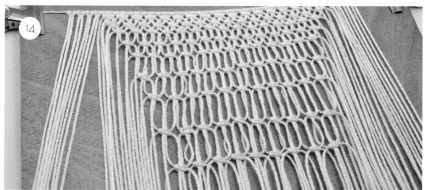

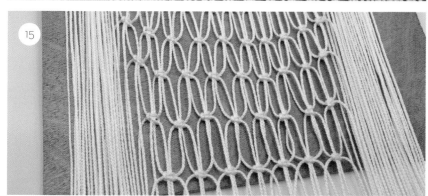

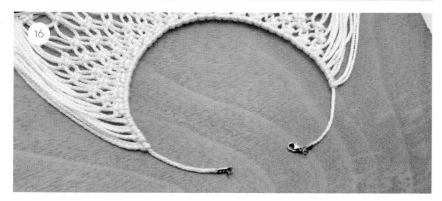

**STEP 5** Repeat step 4 to create a third row of square knots with a small 0.4 in. (1 cm) gap between each line. You have to tie 15 flat knots in this step. (8)

**STEP 6** In the same way, tie two more rows of square knots but this time leave a 0.6 in. (1.5 cm) gap between each line. Then repeat the step twice more to make two more rows, but leaving about a 0.8 in. (2 cm) gap before the new knots and the previous row. Every time you create a new row, you have one knot less to tie. (9, 10, 11, 12)

**STEP 7** Keep repeating the same pattern, slightly enlarging the gaps between each row of square knots. In the pictured example, I made two more rows with 1.4 in. (3.5 cm) gaps, three more with 2 in. (5 cm) gaps, and four final rows with 4 in. (10 cm) gaps. This gives 16 rows in total. You can make more if you want, but the cords will get shorter. (13, 14, 15)

**STEP 8** When the knotting is done, try the necklace on for size and length. Adjust the neck cord until you are happy with the fit, and cut it to your desired length. To fix the crimp clasps, pass the cord ends through and pinch—or glue—them. (16)

**STEP 9** You can cut the cord ends to adjust the fringes to suit you or simply even them up before slightly melting the extremities so the ends don't fray.

# HEADBAND

Headbands go in and out of fashion, but they are always flattering to wear and show a touch of personality in the way they are worn. Aside from style statement, headbands are useful for keeping the hair out of your eyes if you are working or playing outdoors.

**Knots used:**

Diagonal double half hitch knot, overhand knot

**Macramé strands:**

All lengths of brown 3 mm cotton

2 x 48 in. (120 cm)

6 x 67 in. (170 cm)

1 holding strand the width of the board

**Materials:**

Knotting board and clips

Ruler

Scissors

Textile glue

Thin elastic band

**Dimensions:**

You can use any type of cord for this project, although here I have used cotton. This headband is 1.4 in. (3.5 cm) wide, and the lengths of the cords will make it 20 in. (50 cm) long—elastic band not included—but its final length will depend mostly on the types and sizes of cords you use.

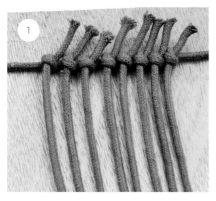

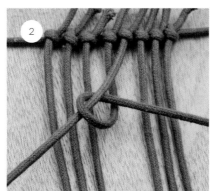

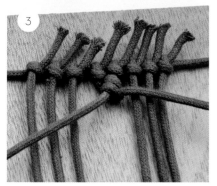

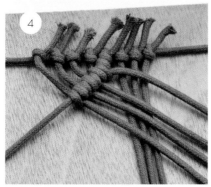

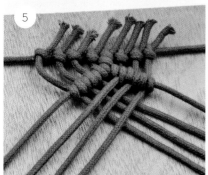

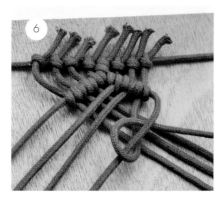

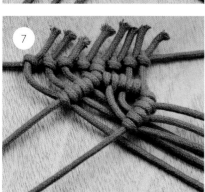

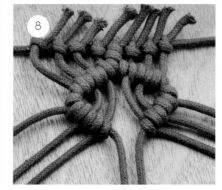

**STEP 1** Clip your holding board thread horizontally. Install both (central) 48 in. (120 cm) strands with simple overhand knots. Leave as little length of cord as possible above the holding thread, since these will be cut off later. On each side of the central cords, place three 67 in. (170 cm) strands, using the same kind of knot. (1)

**STEP 2** Knot together both central threads. Use these same two threads as holding cords on each side, to create a diagonal line of double half hitch knots going from the center to the sides. (2, 3, 4, 5)

**STEP 3** Still using the same two holding cords, tie back the same knotting threads but in reverse order. Hold the cords at an angle that will create a diamond shape once both cords are joined in the next step. (6, 7, 8)

**STEP 4** Repeat from step 2 to step 3 until your headband is long enough. I made 13 diamond shapes, leaving a 4 in. (10 cm) gap at the back of the head to sew the elastic band in the next steps. (9, 10, 11)

**STEP 5** Pull off the holding board thread. Cut the remaining threads on both sides, leaving a short length that you can glue with special textile glue to the backside of your macramé. If you use synthetic cords, you can melt the ends to seal them (see the "Materials" section). (12, 13, 14, 15)

**STEP 6** Cut the elastic band to the desired length. To measure it, try the macramé headband and add 1 in. (2.5 cm) to the length of the gap at the back of your head to make sewing easier later. Pass it through the last diamond shape, making a loop and sewing the elastic sides together to secure. Sew a couple of stitches (see the "Sewing" section) before cutting the excess of elastic. Repeat on the opposite diamond to finish your macramé headband. (16)

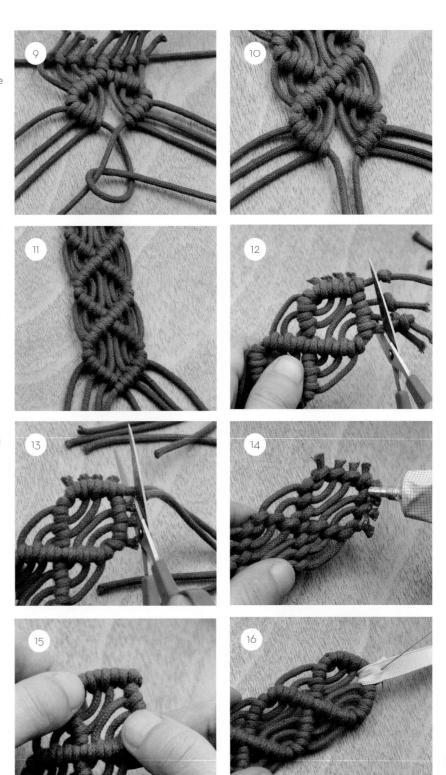

BEGINNER PROJECTS

# FLIP-FLOPS

With this project you can embellish your flip-flops or even repair them if the thong has broken and you want to recycle them. Wear them out and about, and everyone will wonder where you found them!

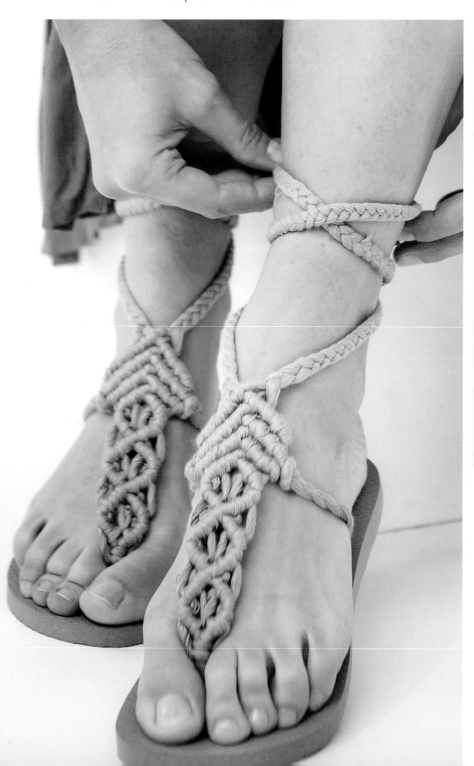

**Knots used:**

Diagonal double half hitch knot, overhand knot, three-strand braid

**Macramé strands:**

All lengths of 4 mm beige cotton thread

For two weavings

4 x 20 in. (50 cm)

8 x 39 in. (100 cm)

2 x 43 in. (110 cm)

2 x 87 in. (220 cm)

**Materials:**

One pair of basic flip-flops

Knotting board and clips

Ruler

Scissors

Textile glue

**Dimensions:**

The instructions given here are to make 16 in. (40 cm) braids to wrap up around your ankles. If you want longer braids to come farther up your legs, replace the 87 in. (220 cm) and the 39 in. (100 cm) cords with longer ones as required.

**STEP 1** Cut off the straps at the base of each flip-flop and clip one of them so as to be able to work on the underside of the sole platform. Pass both 20 in. (50 cm) cords through the front hole and make an overhand knot, using both cords at the same time. This knot needs to be big enough not to slip through, but not so big that it's uncomfortable to walk on. Cut the remaining cords, and you can drop some glue over the knot and hole to seal them in place if desired. (1, 2, 3)

**STEP 2** Unclip the platform and clip it back to work on its upper side. Take one long 87 in. (220 cm) cord, fold it in half, and install it around both short cords with a simple overhand knot. Leave a cord gap between this overhand knot and the platform sole to make the flip-flops more comfortable to wear. Finally, add one 43 in. (110 cm) strand in the same way as before, tying this overhand knot very closely and tightly to the first one. (4, 5)

**STEP 3** Use the left-side 20 in. (50 cm) strand as the holding cord to create a diagonal line and tie double half hitch knots from the center to the left side. Do the same with the three strands on the right side. (6, 7, 8)

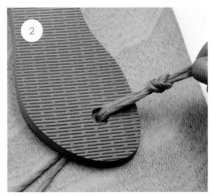

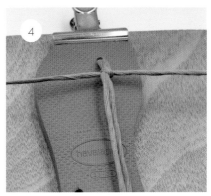

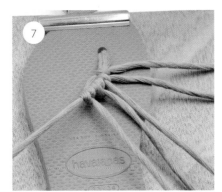

**STEP 4** Use the same holding cords and knot back the same knotting cords tied in the previous step, but in reverse order. These diagonal lines going from the sides to the center will create a kind of diamond shape when you join them in the middle with a last double half hitch knot. Be sure your holding cords are held at the right angle. Repeat step 3 and step 4 twice more to create three diamond shapes. (9, 10)

**STEP 5** Install two 39 in. (100 cm) cords inside each hole as before in step 1. Roll each pair of cords together and secure these two-strand braids with a simple—but tight—overhand knot. I usually make these braids 3 in. (8 cm) long, but you can adjust them by putting your foot in the sandal and checking that the last diamond shape and both braids connect well without becoming too tight—but not too loose either. (11)

**STEP 6** Make a diagonal line to join both parts together by using one of the left braid strands as the holding cord and the three left strands of the diamond shape as knotting cords. Do the same on the opposite side and join both holding cords in the middle. Repeat this step with the second threads (of the braids) to create a second line on each side. (12, 13, 14)

**STEP 7** Create a third line on each side with the next right and next left cords. Once these steps are completed, the shortest strands should be the two farthest right and two farthest left. Make sure of this before braiding the three long threads left on each side. For this demonstration I have made two 16 in. (40 cm) long braids (see page 24); you can adjust these lengths depending on the size of your ankle and how high up your leg you want the braids to go. At the end of each braid, make a tight overhand knot to secure it. (15, 16)

**STEP 8** Cut both short threads on each side, leaving each cord about 0.5 in. (1 cm) long. These are then glued on the underside of your weaving. Cut the remaining cords after the overhand knots at the end of the braids. (17, 18, 19, 20)

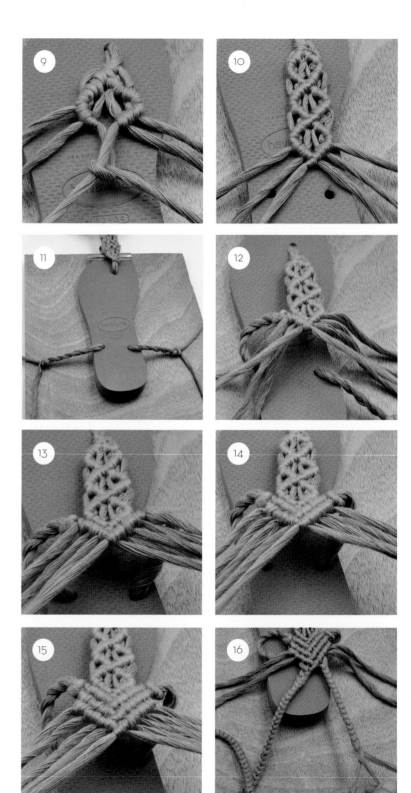

# INTERMEDIATE
# PROJECTS

# WIDE CUFF

Transform a favorite shirt by adding eye-catching wide cuffs. Choose a selection of contrasting shades or go all-out with a blaze of different colors.

**Knots used:**

Diagonal double half hitch knot, lark's head knot, overhand knot

**Macramé strands:**

All lengths of 1 mm waxed thread. Amounts for 2 cuffs.

4 x Straw, 40 in. (100 cm)

6 x Straw, 80 in. (200 cm)

8x Dark gray, 80 in. (200 cm)

16 x White, 80 in. (200 cm)

16 x Light gray, 80 in. (200 cm)

1 holding board strand, the width of the board

**Materials:**

1 shirt with wide, stiff cuffs

8 x small sew-on snap fasteners

Knotting board and clips

Needle and white sewing thread/cord

Ruler and lighter

Scissors

**Dimensions:**

Each cuff is 3 in. (7.5 cm) wide and 6.75 in. (17 cm) long. You can change this by allowing about 24 in. (60 cm) of threads (12 in. for both shorter lengths) to create 2 in. (5 cm) of macramé weaving.

**STEP 1** Secure the holding board thread horizontally with your clips—the thread color does not matter. Take the four dark gray threads, fold them in half, and knot them onto the board strand using lark's head knots. On both sides, successively install one light gray and one white thread. Follow this with three 80 in. (200 cm) straw strands between each white—still using lark's head knots. Then, finally, one 40 in. (100 cm) straw strand on each side, using simple overhand knots. (1, 2)

**STEP 2** Start working with the farthest-left 12 threads. Knot the two dark gray cords together with a diagonal double half hitch knot and use them as holding cords to create one line on each side with the next five cords. (3, 4, 5)

**STEP 3** Repeat step 2 three times, always working with 12-strand groups, until you reach the right-hand side. Join together the dark gray strands between each group of threads. (6, 7, 8)

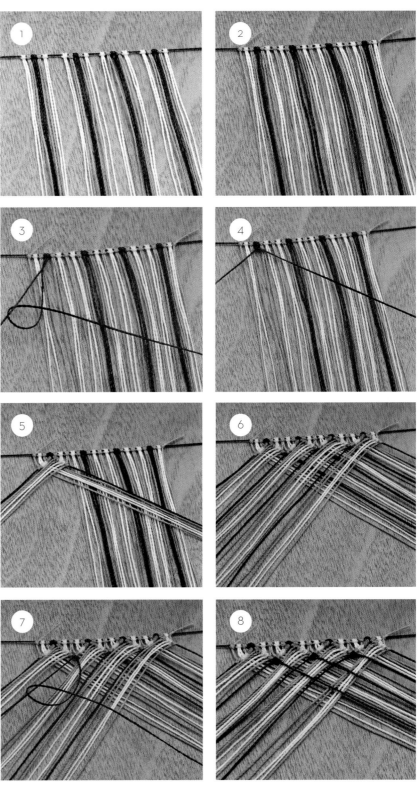

**STEP 4** Return to the first group of strands. Repeat step 2 by tying both central light gray threads and use them as holding cords to create a line on each side with the next five strands. Repeat this step with every group of cords until you reach the right-hand side of the weaving. Don't forget to tie the farthest-left and farthest-right dark gray cords (coming out from the first lines) and knot together the light gray strands between each group. (9, 10, 11, 12)

**STEP 5** Keep making lines as before, but take care that your diagonal lines start and finish in a staggered pattern. To check that you haven't made a mistake, note that by line 6, the colors and threads should be back to their original positions. Keep repeating the pattern over and over until your cuff gets to the desired length. (13, 14)

**STEP 6** Pull off the holding board strand. Cut, then carefully and neatly melt the cords ends on both sides. (15)

**STEP 7** Using white cord, sew the undersides of four snaps under the macramé weaving. To keep the sewing as invisible as possible, place them on the white parts of your macramé. (16)

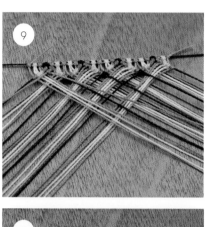
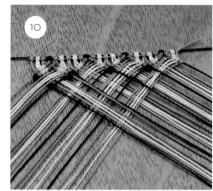
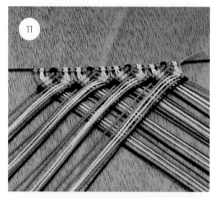
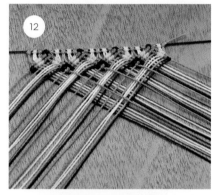
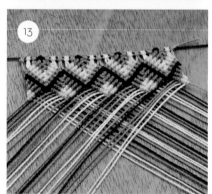
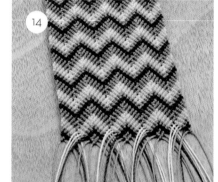
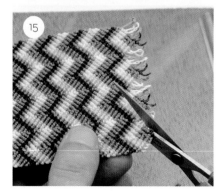

**STEP 8** Repeat all the steps to make an identical cuff. (17)

**Attaching your Macramé**

Sew the upper part of the snap fasteners on your shirt cuffs. Take the time to carefully align them with the ones on your macramé weaving before sewing them in place. (18)

# LONG JACKET STRIP

I was inspired to design this particularly long strip by a macramé friendship bracelet I once saw. It provides a really original touch to your classic jacket, thanks to its striking zigzag pattern. The great thing about this design is that you can embellish any kind of clothing or accessory simply by adjusting its length and coloring.

**Knots used:**

Diagonal double half hitch knot, flat square knot, overhand knot, vertical double half hitch knot

**Macramé strands:**

All lengths of 1 mm waxed threads

2 x Teal, 83 in. (210 cm)

10 x Teal, 124 in. (315 cm)

1 x Light brown, 275 in. (700 cm)

1 holding board strand, the width of the board

**Materials:**

1 straight jacket with zip

Knotting board and clips

Needle and teal blue sewing thread/cord

Ruler and lighter

Scissors

**Dimensions:**

The width of the weaving is 0.8 in. (2 cm), and it measures approximately 27 in. (70 cm) long. If you want to make it longer or shorter, for every 4 in. (10 cm) strip, you need two teal blue threads measuring 12 in. (30 cm), plus 10 more measuring 18 in. (45 cm), and finally one 40 in. (100 cm) light brown thread.

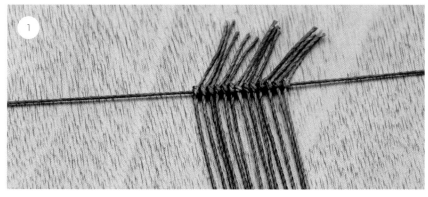

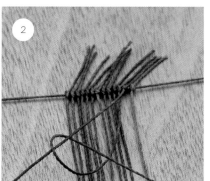

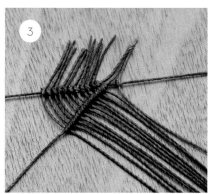

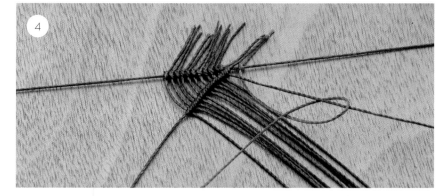

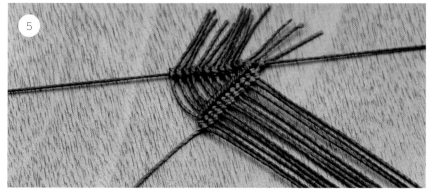

**STEP 1** Clip the holding board strand horizontally across your board—the color doesn't matter—and install the light brown strand with a simple overhand knot. On the left and still using simple overhand knots, place both 83 in. (210 cm) blue threads and all the other blue threads. (1)

**STEP 2** Tie both the 83 in. (210 cm) blue strands together with a double half hitch knot. Holding the farthest-right strand at a diagonal, and using it as the holding cord, tie every other blue strand to create a line going from right to left. (2, 3)

**STEP 3** Taking the brown cord as the knotting cord, tie it around each blue strand with vertical double half hitch knots. At the end of the line, knot the cord coming out from the first line in the same way as you tied the others. (4, 5)

**STEP 4** Return to the right side. Use the first blue cord to create another line exactly as before in step 2. This second blue line must be knotted tightly up against the brown knotted line. At the end of the line, tie the brown strand with the blue ones exactly the same way as before. (6)

**STEP 5** Make a square knot with two holding threads inside the knot, using the four farthest-right strands. Make a second square knot (again with two strands inside), using the two nearest-left strands, plus two of the strands used previously, to make the first square knot. Repeat this twice to get a row of four square knots. At the end of this step you should have two blue cords left: one that was not used to make the row of four knots, and one coming out from the blue line made in step 4. (7, 8, 9, 10, 11)

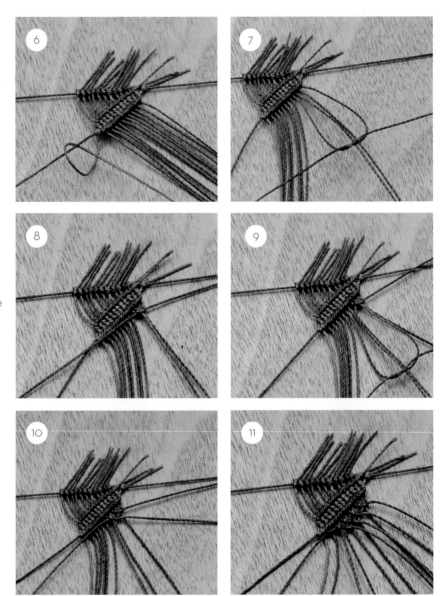

**STEP 6** Return to the right side and repeat the previous step, but this time make a row of three square knots. Be very careful not to tie the first square knot too tightly—you need to leave a cord gap on its right. If you tie it too hard, this side of the weaving will start to curve instead of staying flat. (12)

**STEP 7** Make a row of two square knots, repeating the last step. Again, don't tie the first knot too tightly. Finish this step by making a last (not too tight) square knot to complete the triangular shape. (13, 14)

**STEP 8** Take the blue thread not used to make the row of four square knots in step 5 (the one perpendicular to the blue line), and use it as the holding cord to make a line going from left to right. To do this, knot every blue cord on its right side and make sure the line is tight up against the square-knotted triangle shape. Be careful here! It's easy to miss a blue cord while making the line. To see if you missed one, turn over the weaving and check the underside. (15, 16)

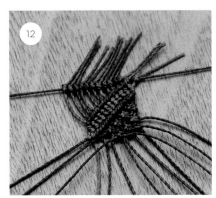
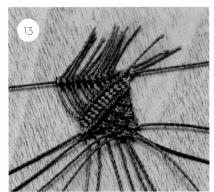
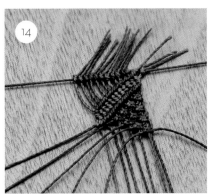
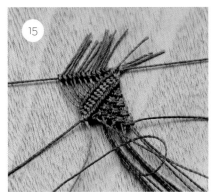
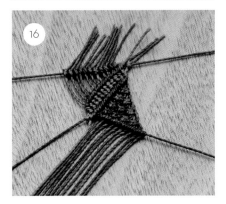

**STEP 9** Repeat step 3, but this time work from left to right using the brown cord to make another brown row of vertical knots all along the blue line. When you reach the end of the line don't forget to knot the blue cord coming out from the blue line. Finally, repeat step 4 again, working on the opposite side. (17, 18)

**STEP 10** Repeat steps, 5, 6, 7 to create another square knot triangle shape, but this time on the left side of your weaving. Always start the first square knot of each row with the four furthest left strands. (19)

**STEP 11** Repeat step 8 in the opposite direction—working from right to left—to create a line all along the triangle shape. Now return to step 3 and repeat for as many times as you need to get the length you need. At the end of your weaving be sure the brown line finishes on the right side of your knotting. This will give a better finish when you add the strip to your jacket. (20, 21, 22). Unclip your holding board cord and pull it off. Cut and carefully melt all the remaining strands on both sides. (23, 24)

**Attaching your Macramé**

For this project finely stitch your macramé to the jacket using a matching color thread. (25)

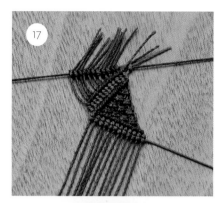
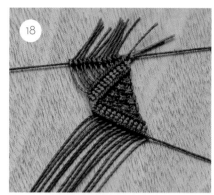
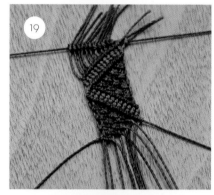
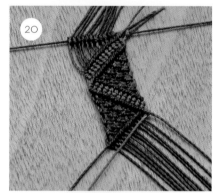
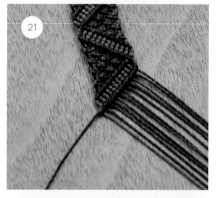
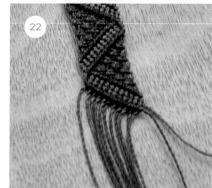

# Sandal Anklets

Decorative anklets really belong to carefree sunny days. Customize your own and enjoy summer on the beach or in the town with these easy and attractive sandals.

**Knots used:**

Horizontal diagonal double half hitch knot, lark's head knot, overhand knot, spiral square knot, vertical double half hitch knot

**Macramé strands:**

All lengths of 1 mm waxed thread (for two anklets):

16 x Black, 79 in. (200 cm)

6 x Black, 16 in. (40 cm)

8 x Brown, 16 in. (40 cm)

4 x Orange, 16 in. (40 cm)

2 x Black, 8 in. (20 cm)

**Materials:**

1 pair of sandals with ankles straps

About 100 x 3 mm glass beads

Knotting board and clips

Needle and black sewing cord

Ruler and lighter

Scissors

**Dimensions:**

These macramé anklets measure 1 in. (2.5 cm) at their thinnest and 2 in. (5 cm) in the middle, where the beads sit. The cord lengths given here are to make an 8 in. (20 cm) weaving. If you need them longer, replace the 79 in. (200 cm) cords with longer lengths, and tie more rows of vertical knots in step 4 and step 11.

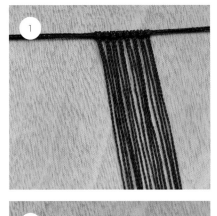

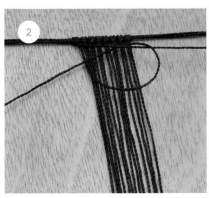

**STEP 1** Clip the three 16 in. (40 cm) strands onto your board. Place eight 79 in. (200 cm) cords by folding them in the middle and then tying with lark's head knots. Once installed, make sure they are sitting in the middle of the clipped cords. (1)

**STEP 2** Use the left-hand strand as the holding cord. Make a horizontal line tying the next seven threads with double half hitch knots. Do the same on the opposite side, using the first right-hand thread as the holding cord. Join both holding cords with a last knot when they meet in the middle. (2, 3, 4)

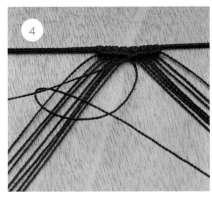

**STEP 3** Tie the strands in pairs, making one vertical double half hitch knot with each pair of cords. You need to tie four knots on each side—the left-side knots are made from left to right, and the right-side ones from right to left. Finally, repeat step 2 to make a line on each side of your weaving. (5, 6)

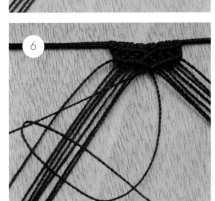

**STEP 4** Repeat step 3 ten more times to finally get 11 rows of vertical knots. If you're using longer strands, you can knot more rows to make your anklet longer. (7)

**STEP 5** Take one light brown strand and begin an overhand knot on one end without tying it. Pass the farthest-left thread through the prepared knot, then tie it tightly up against the previous line. Add a simple vertical half-hitch knot to completely fix the strand. Then knot all of the next seven with full vertical double half hitch knots. (8, 9)

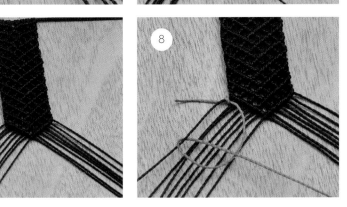

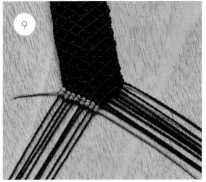

**STEP 6** Working on the right side, repeat step 5. Join both knotting cords together when they meet in the middle. Then repeat step 2 to create a plain line, but instead of knotting seven cords on each side, tie eight of them together, including the brown cord. (10, 11)

**STEP 7** Repeat steps 5 and 6 twice more, using orange and then brown strands. (12)

**STEP 8** Working from the center, knot the second strands—the brown ones—using double half hitch knots around both central cords. Thread a bead onto each of the next cords on either side before knotting them around the first (already tied) black holding cord. In the same way, knot the next orange strands but without adding any beads. Continue the same technique, beading only one cord of the two. I used three beads for the second bead row, four for the third, six for the fourth, and eight for the last one, but you can adjust the quantity of beads depending on their sizes. (13, 14, 15, 16)

**STEP 9** Knot both central brown cords together and keep tying them with vertical double half hitch knots until you reach the sides of your macramé. Don't forget to also knot the cords coming out from the last line you made. Then knot both central black cords and, using them as holding cords, make a plain line with diagonal double half hitch knots from the center to both sides. When you reach the end of these lines, do not tie the brown cords—leave them on the sides; they will be cut later. (17)

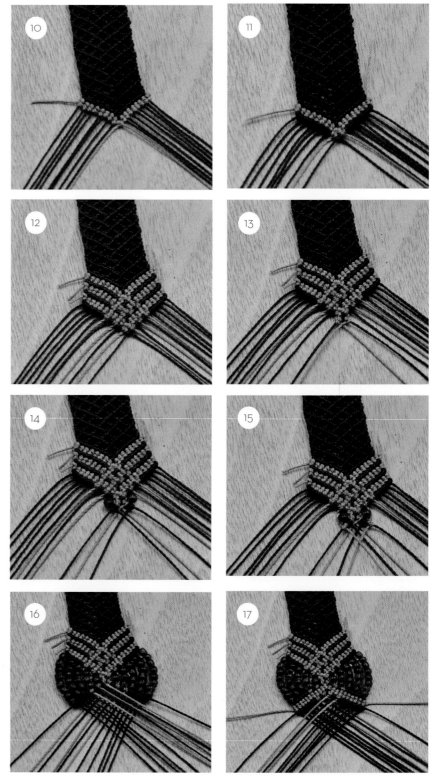

**STEP 10** Repeat the previous step twice, using the orange strands, and then again with the brown. (18)

**STEP 11** As before in step 3, tie your strands in pairs with vertical knots, but this time, on the left side of the macramé, make knots running from right to left, and on the right-side knots from left to right. Then knot both central threads and, using them as holding cords, make a diagonal line on each side. Repeat this step 10 times—or more if necessary—to get 11 rows of vertical knots. (19, 20, 21)

**STEP 12** Continue with the same holding cords and tie back the same knotting strands (but in reverse order) to create a diamond shape when both holding cords are joined in the middle. Don't forget to hold these cords at the right angle to create a diamond shape. Complete this step by making a line on both sides (as knotted before in step 2). (22)

**STEP 13** Unclip your anklet. Clip it back upside down to make two three-strand braids, using the previously clipped strands. In this project I made them 5 in. (13 cm) long, but you can adjust their length depending on your foot size. Remember, the result needs to be long enough for you to pass your foot through the anklet once the sliding knot is made. (23)

**STEP 14** Cut and melt every remaining cord. You can add one or more beads at the end of your braids, cutting and melting only two cords out of three. Then repeat every step from step 1 to step 14 to create a second anklet. (24)

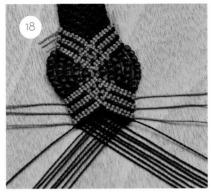
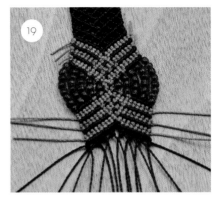
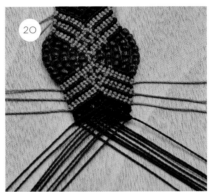
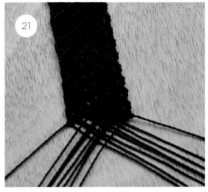
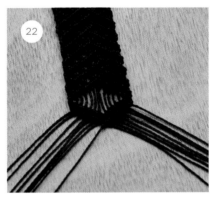
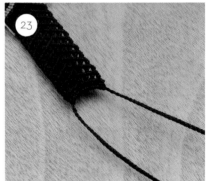

**STEP 15** Take the 8 in. (20 cm) cord and make an overhand knot, but without tightening it. Pass both braids inside the diamond shape, and then through the prepared knot before tying it securely. Make a few spiral square knots, using the braids as holding cords, and cut the remaining threads on both sides of the sliding knot. (25, 26)

**Attaching your Macramé**

Sew your anklets onto the sandal straps, being careful to place them so that the decorative center sits right in the middle of your ankle. To get this exact, try the anklets on and dot the exact point with a pen. Sew them on by using a few firm stitches, making sure the beads are centrally placed so you can easily close the straps. Do not make stitches on the sides of the anklet. (27)

# BELT

A colorful macramé belt is an invaluable accessory and hugely adaptable for many different looks. Worn loose and casual, it is a fashion and lifestyle statement that says, "I'm cool." Worn tightly cinched, it holds up your pants!

**Knots used:**

Horizontal double half hitch knot, lark's head knot, Vertical double half hitch knot

**Macramé strands:**

All lengths of 1 mm waxed thread

13 x White, 70 in. (180 cm)

Mixed colors, between 6 and 23 in. (15-60 cm)

(I used white, golden, gray, light, and dark brown)

1 holding board strand, the width of the board

**Materials:**

One 1.5 in. (4 cm) wide belt buckle

1 chopstick (or similar shaped object)

Knotting board and clips

Ruler and lighter

Scissors

**Dimensions:**

The strand length given here is to make a belt measuring 1.5 in. (4 cm) wide and 33 in. (85 cm) long. You can easily change the width by using a smaller or bigger buckle and adjusting the quantity of white cords you install in step 1. The length can be modified by altering the length of the white cords; the best way to calculate this is to measure your waist size, add 4 in. (10 cm), then multiply the result by 2.

**STEP 1** Secure the belt buckle on your board using the holding board strand. Install the 70 in. (180 cm) white threads directly on the buckle: fold the thread in half and use lark's head knots. You can alter the number of strands as necessary, but make sure your weaving will be able to pass easily through the inner buckle once the belt is done. (1)

**STEP 2** Take one 16 in. (40 cm) color strand and knot it with a simple overhand knot onto the first left-side white thread. Then make a simple vertical half hitch knot on the same white strand to fix it. (2, 3, 4)

**STEP 3** Working from left to right, make a full colored row with vertical double half hitch knots. Knot each white strand until the row is completed to the right edge. Throughout the weaving, you have to make vertical knots from side to side. (5)

**STEP 4** Take a 23 in. (60 cm) cord, and as before in step 2, prepare an overhand knot on its end without tying it, and pass the farthest-right white strand through it before closing it. Make a simple vertical half hitch knot on the same strand to fix it, and continue knotting it around the next white cord in turn as you did with the first color, but this time working from right to left. (6)

**STEP 5** When the second row is complete, keep using the same knotting cord to make more vertical knots, but this time from left to right until your strand get too short to be tied. Add a new color strand on the next white thread, the same way as in step 2. When you knot it, be sure its starting end is hidden under the weaving, because it will be cut later. Keep making vertical knots until you reach the right edge. If your strand is long enough, make more knots from right to left with the same thread. (7, 8)

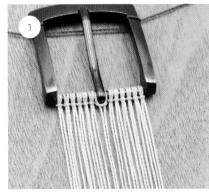
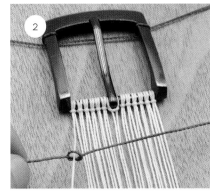
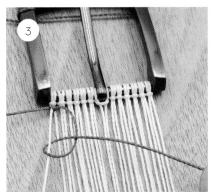
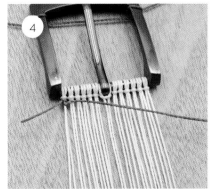

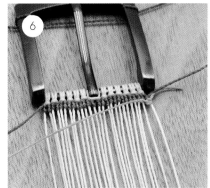
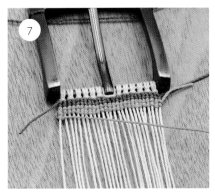
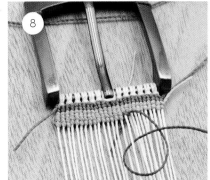

**STEP 6** Continue repeating the previous steps with various colored threads and sizes until the belt is the length of your waist. To make the colors appear random and create a camouflage effect, vary the starting and finishing points of the different colors. (9, 10, 11)

**STEP 7** When you reach the last 4in (10cm) of your macramé belt you have to create small holes in the middle of the weaving to be able to close the buckle. To do this, keep making colored rows from one side to the other, but without knotting both central white holding cords on two rows in eight (to leave small holes). For this, pass the knotting thread under both center holding cords, then keep knotting the next holding thread. When you have made two rows without knotting these central cords, keep making normal rows until you reach the position where you want to create the next hole. (12, 13, 14)

**STEP 8** When your belt is long enough, secure the last row taking the furthest left white thread as the holding cord, to make a line with horizontal double half hitch knots to the center of the knotting. Repeat from the opposite side, starting with the furthest right white thread. Join both holding cords together at the center with a final knot. Repeat this step two more times to finally get three white lines. (15, 16, 17)

**STEP 9** Finish your macramé belt by cutting and melting all the threads that remain on the sides, as well as underneath the weaving. Finally use a chopstick—or any similar long tapering object—to spread the white holding cords and shape the holes. (18, 19)

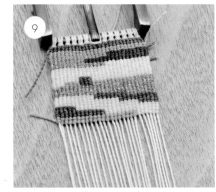
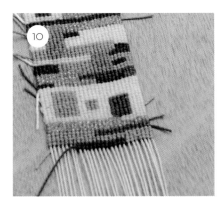
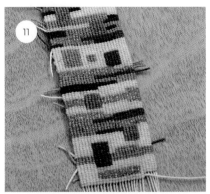
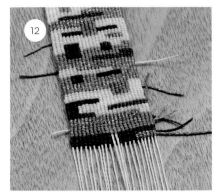
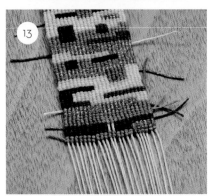
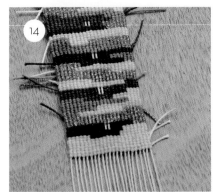
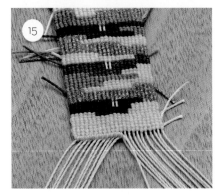
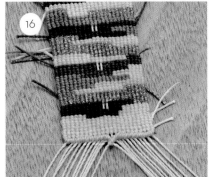

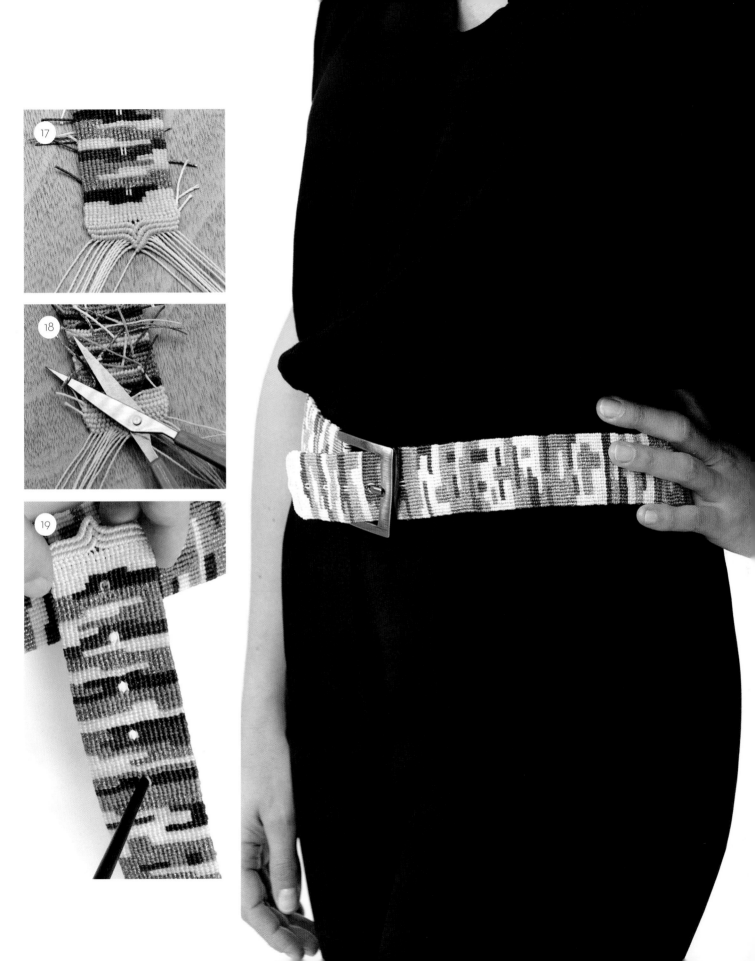

# Banana Bag Strap

Personalize your banana bag—or any other type of carrier bag—with this wide macramé cotton rope strap. Its comfortable width would even make a great guitar strap or any similar type of carrying or support handle.

**Knots used:**

Diagonal double half hitch knot, flat square knot, overhand knot, spiral square knot, vertical double half hitch knot

**Macramé strands:**

2 mm White cotton cords

30 x 138 in. (350 cm) lengths

1 holding board strand, the width of the board

**Materials:**

One banana bag with openable rings or small side carabiners

2 x 3 in. (8 cm) metal rings

Knotting board and clips

Ruler

Scissors

**Dimensions:**

The width of this macramé strap is 3 in. (8 cm), and it measures 27 in. (70 cm) long, excluding the rings and fringes. If you want to change the length, you can easily modify it by using longer cords and making longer rows of spiral and flat square knots.

**STEP 1** Secure one ring with the holding board thread. Using simple but tight overhand knots, tie your cords in groups of three on the lower side of the ring, leaving approximately 14 in. (35 cm) of cord above it. You don't need to be very precise here, because at the end you will cut them to even up both fringes. (1)

**STEP 2** Separate the strands into two equal groups. Take the farthest-left and farthest-right threads to use as holding cords. Make two lines from each side to the center, using diagonal double half hitch knots and join them in the middle. (2, 3, 4)

**STEP 3** Repeat step 2 three more times, to make four diagonal lines on each side. (5)

**STEP 4** Work with the six central strands. Using the two outer cords as knotting cords (leaving four strands inside the knots), make a 3 in. (8 cm) row of spiral square knots. Then do the same on each side, using four strands to create each row, but this time leave two threads inside the knots. Make three 3 in. (8 cm) rows of spiral square knots. (6, 7, 8)

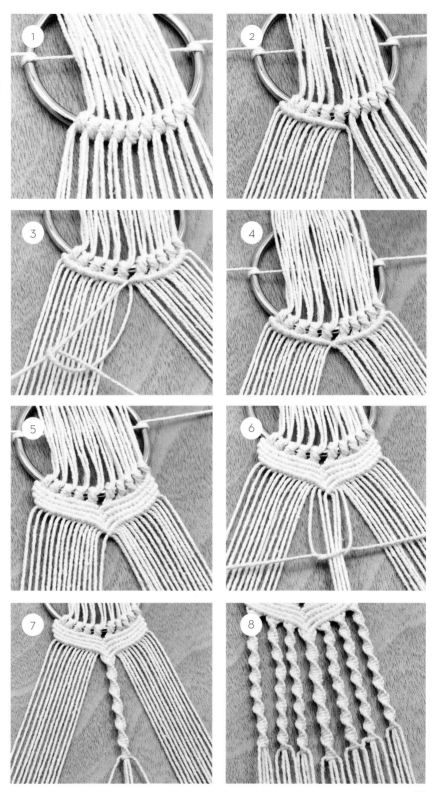

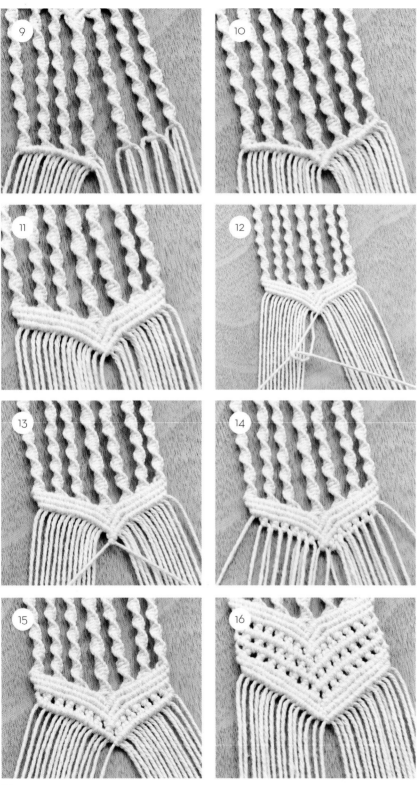

**STEP 5** As before in step 2, separate all the strands into two groups and use the farthest-left and farthest-right cords to make two lines with double half hitch knots. Join them at the center. Repeat twice more to get three lines on each side. (9, 10, 11)

**STEP 6** Keep separating your strands into two groups. Knot them in pairs and work from the center to the sides, making one vertical double half hitch knot with each pair of threads. When you've finished, you should have seven vertical knots, plus one strand left on each side. Use these unused strands as holding cords to make a line going from the side to the center. Join them together where they meet. (12, 13, 14, 15)

**STEP 7** Repeat step 6 twice more so that you have three rows of vertical knots. Add two more diagonal lines (as before in step 2) to finally make three lines. (16)

**STEP 8** Repeat step 4, but make seven 2 in. (5 cm) rows of flat square knots (instead of 3 in. (8 cm) spiral square knots). Don't forget to put four cords inside the middle square knot's row, and two in the sides ones. (17)

**STEP 9** Repeat from step 5 to step 8. Then, after weaving your second row of flat square knots, repeat step 5 one last time to create three more lines. (18, 19)

**STEP 10** Use both center cords as holding cords to make a single diagonal line out to each side. These lines must be knotted from the last lines made in the previous step. However, to do so you have to adjust the angle of the holding cords and the firmness of your knots. Using the same holding cords, complete the step by making one more line on each side, but this time work from the sides to the center at an angle that will make a diamond shape when they are joined in the middle. (20, 21)

**STEP 11** Now repeat the weaving, but in the opposite direction so as to get a symmetrical strap. Repeat the first part of step 10, three times, to create three lines going from the center out to the sides. (22, 23)

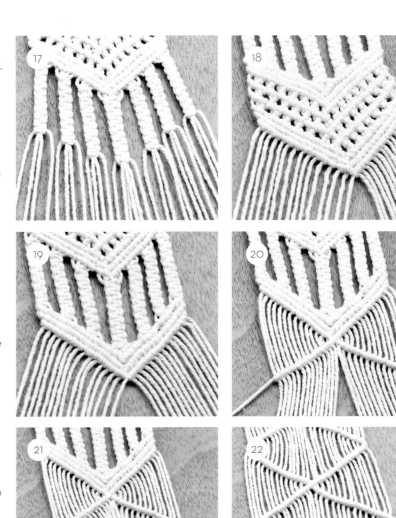

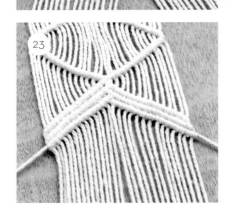

**STEP 12** Repeat step 8, to create seven rows of flat square knots, then repeat step 11. (24, 25)

**STEP 13** Repeat steps 6 and 7, but leaving out the farthest-left and farthest-right strands. Make vertical pairs of knots with all the other threads. The only difference is that when you make the plain diagonal lines between each row of vertical knots, you have to make them from the center out to the sides, using both the central cords as holding cords. (26)

**STEP 14** Repeat both of the last steps, but be careful here. As you'll notice, some cords get shorter than others as the weaving progresses. To rebalance their length, use the longest cords to make flat square knot rows, and leave the shortest ones inside the knots. Do this for each group of four cords—and the six-cord group in the middle; if you don't, you may find your strap running short on some cords, while there's too much length on others. (27)

**STEP 15** Still using the longest cords, repeat step 4 to make spiral square knots. Complete the piece with three final lines running from the center out to the sides. (28)

**STEP 16** Finish your strap by adding the second ring the same way as the first ring, by tying the cords in groups of three with overhand knots. Depending on how you want the strap to look, you can cut the fringes as long or short as you want to make a neat finish, or leave them uneven to accentuate the boho look. Up to you! You can also challenge your skills by dip-dyeing a part of the fringe cords to give a touch of color to your strap. (29)

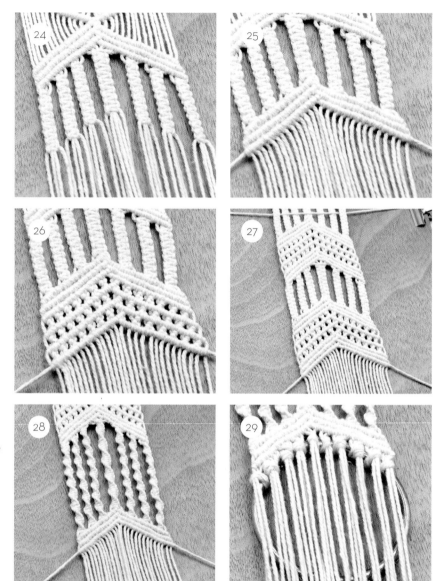

### Attaching the Macramé

In case your rings are not openable and you need to join two of them to connect your strap to your bag, you can create your own macramé ring. To do so, weave a 1 in. (2.5 cm) flat square knot strip, leaving about 3 in. (8 cm) of holding cord at the beginning and at the end of your strip. Once your weaving is done, cut and melt the knotting cord ends and finally tie both holding-cord extremities with a tight double overhand knot, enclosing both metal rings inside the macramé circle before cutting and melting the holding-cord leftovers.

# Fringed Choker Necklace

This black statement necklace adds understated drama and elegance to any simple blouse or dress.

**Knots used:**

Diagonal double half hitch knot, spiral square knot, three-strand braid

**Macramé strands:**

All lengths of 1 mm waxed thread

100 x Black, 35 in. (90 cm)

9 x Black, 39 in. (100 cm)

1 x Black, 12 in. (30 cm)

**Materials:**

Knotting board and clips

Scissors

Ruler and lighter

**Dimensions:**

The macramé triangle shape is about 5 in. (13 cm) wide and 2.5 in. (6.5 cm) deep. At the middle the fringes measure approximatively 6 in. (15 cm) long, but they can easily be adjusted, depending on how much of a statement you want to make.

**STEP 1** This project is knotted in groups of 10 strands at a time. Start by clipping together the nine 39 in. (100 cm) threads on your board. These cords will be used later to make the braids that go around the neck. At this point you can adjust the number of strands if you want to make the neck braids thinner or thicker.

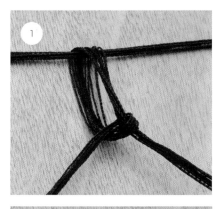

**STEP 2** Take ten 35 in. (90 cm) strands together and, using them as a single cord, pass them under the nine holding cords. Fold this cord in the middle and make a diagonal double half hitch knot (as shown in the photo). Be sure that your knot falls in the center of the clipped strands. Once the first big knot is made, repeat the step four more times, working leftward, but leaving a small gap between each knot. (1, 2, 3)

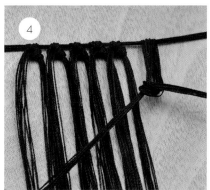

**STEP 3** Repeat step 2 on the right side with five more 10-strand groups, but making double half hitch knots in the opposite direction. You will finally get 20 groups of 10 strands to work with. (4, 5)

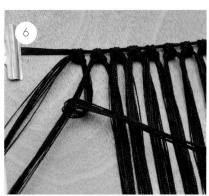

**STEP 4** Starting with the left group, leave the first cord alone and make a knot, using the second cord as the knotting thread and the third one as the holding thread. Tie three more big knots, each time using the next two groups of strands to the right. This will result in four knots going in the same direction. Repeat this step with the 10 right-side cords, making knots in the opposite (left) direction. (6, 7, 8, 9)

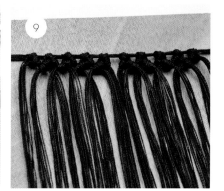

**STEP 5** Now work with the four central cords: cross both center groups, passing the left cord under and then above the right one, and knot it around the next group to its left side. Then tie the second crossed group around the next group of strands to its right side. This way you will join together both sides of your weaving. (10, 11, 12, 13)

**STEP 6** As shown in the photo, tie three more knots on each side of your knotting, in the same direction you did in the previous step. (14)

**STEP 7** Leaving alone both central groups, tie three knots on each side between each knot made previously. Be sure to make them perpendicular to the ones in the above row. (15)

**STEP 8** Repeat from step 5 to step 7, but once you have crossed and tied both central groups, make only two more knots on each side (instead of the three for both last steps). (16, 17)

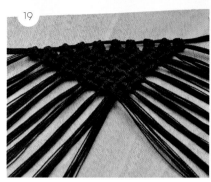

**STEP 9** Repeat step 8, but this time tying only one knot on each side after both central groups are crossed and knotted, plus one perpendicular knot on each side underneath. Then cross and knot the two groups in the middle again and make a final double half hitch knot with both last holding-strand groups. This completes the triangle shape. (18, 19, 20)

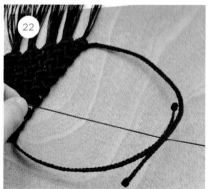

**STEP 10** Unclip your weaving, then clip it back so that you can make one braid on each side, using the nine strands installed in step 1. I make them 12 in. (30 cm) long and plait them simply as if I was doing three-strand braids, but you can make them as long as you like. Just be sure you'll be able to pass your head through them once the sliding knot is done. Tie an overhand knot at their ends to secure them before cutting and melting the leftover cords just above the knot. (21)

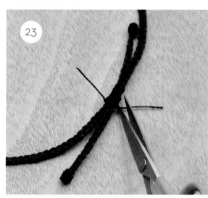

**STEP 11** To create the sliding knot, take the 12 in. (30 cm) thread and prepare an overhand knot in its middle, without tying it. Pass both braids through this knot, tie it, and make a few spiral square knots before cutting and melting both cords remaining on the sides. Finish your necklace by neatening the fringe length. (22, 23)

# Yoga Shirt Backstrap

Make the back of your yoga (or indeed any other) shirt totally bespoke with this unusual decorative but subtle and totally feminine strapping.

**Knots used:**

Flat square knot, horizontal diagonal double half hitch knot, lark's head knot, spiral square knot, vertical double half hitch knot

**Macramé strands:**

12 x 110 in. (280 cm) lengths of black 1 mm waxed thread
1 holding board strand the width of the board

**Materials:**

One T-back (or Y-back) tank top
Knotting board and clips
Needle and black sewing thread/cord
Ruler and lighter
Scissors

**Dimensions:**

For the best result, your T- or Y-shaped tank top needs to have a specific size. The width of the shoulder braces has to measure about 0.75 in. (2 cm), and the principal back middle brace needs to be about 1.5 in. (4 cm) wide.

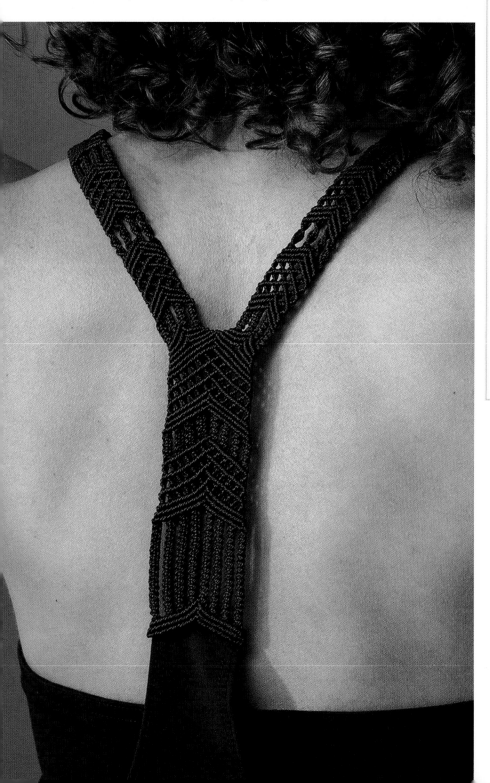

**STEP 1** Note that this project starts upside down and works from the wide bottom up to the shoulder braces. Clip the holding thread—its color doesn't matter—to your board. Fold in half every black strand and install them onto the holding cord with lark's head knots. (1)

**STEP 2** Separate your strands into two equal groups. Take the farthest-left and farthest-right threads and, using them as holding cords, knot horizontal double half hitch knots, making one line on each side. Join both lines when they meet in the middle. Repeat this step twice more to end up with three lines on each side. (2, 3, 4)

**STEP 3** Working with the strands in threes, create eight rows of flat square knots—four on each side—each measuring about 1.5 in. (4 cm). Then join the rows of flat square knots together by repeating step 2. (5, 6, 7)

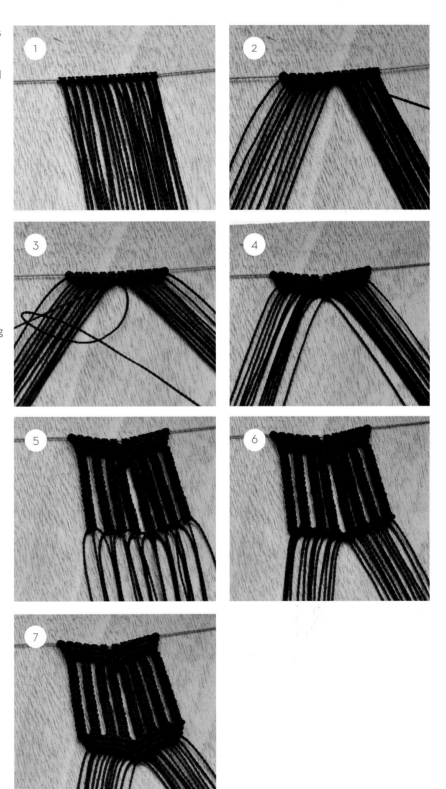

**STEP 4** Tie the strands in pairs with vertical double half hitch knots, starting from the sides and working inward to the center. This means making six knots on each side. Create a line on each side with the farthest-left and farthest-right cords (as before in step 2), before joining them in the middle. Repeat this step twice more. (8, 9, 10)

**STEP 5** Remake step 3, but this time make them in rows of about 0.5 in. (1 cm) flat square knots. Repeat step 4, and finally step 2. On completion you should have three lines on each side. (11, 12, 13)

**STEP 6** The goal now is to separate your work into two weavings to create the Y shape. To do so, work on each side separately. With the 12 left-side strands, repeat step 2 and knot three small lines. Do the same with the 12 right-side strands. (14)

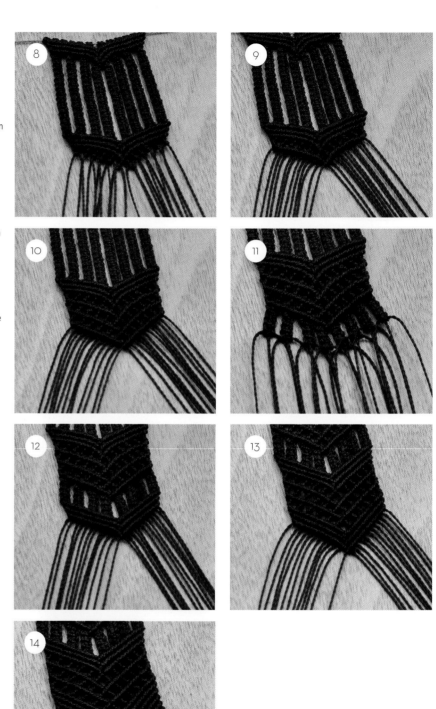

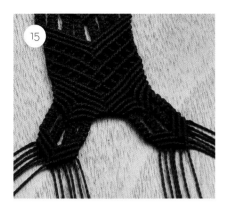

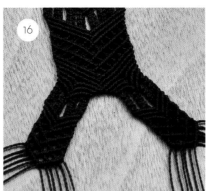

**STEP 7** As before, make rows of 0.5 in. (1 cm) flat square knots, followed by three plain diagonal lines. Repeat step 4, making three vertical double half hitch knots on each side of each knotting. (15, 16)

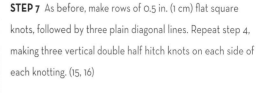

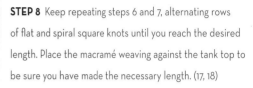

**STEP 8** Keep repeating steps 6 and 7, alternating rows of flat and spiral square knots until you reach the desired length. Place the macramé weaving against the tank top to be sure you have made the necessary length. (17, 18)

**STEP 9** Pull the holding board strand from your macramé knotting. Cut and melt all the remaining cords on every side. (19, 20)

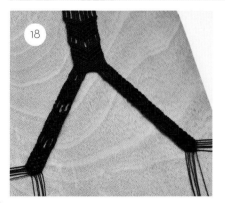

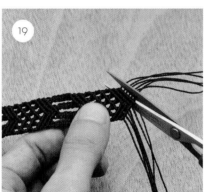

**STEP 10** It's now time to cut away the T (or Y) back of your tank top. Cut it, leaving about 1 in. (2.5 cm) of fabric overlap under each end of your macramé knotting. This will make fixing easier. (21)

**Attaching your Macramé**

For this project, finely stitch your macramé in position, using a matching color thread. Once it's secure, cut off any excess fabric underneath. That's it, finished. Time for that yoga class! (22)

21

22

# ADVANCED
# PROJECTS

# MACRAMÉ TIARA

Discover your inner princess with this unusual macramé tiara. It's ideal for parties and special occasions—worn with your hair either up or down—to add color and sophistication to your outfit. Or just wear it out and about to get yourself noticed!

**Knots used:**

Horizontal diagonal double half hitch knot, lark's head knot, overhand knot, spiral square knot, three-strand braid, vertical double half hitch knot

**Macramé strands:**

All lengths of 1 mm brick red waxed thread

16 x 79 in. (200 cm)

8 x 43 in. (110 cm)

8 x 90 in. (230 cm)

1 holding board strand, the width of the board

**Materials:**

Knotting board and clips

Needle

Ruler and lighter

Scissors

**Dimensions:**

The width of the tiara is 2 in. (5 cm), and it's 13 in. (33 cm) long, but this is adjustable thanks to the sliding knot. It is made in three different pieces: the two that make up the base of the tiara are the same knotting but a different width. The third piece is made up of a strip of overlapping squares.

**Part 1: Base sections**

**STEP 1** To make the base, start at the widest, flattest part of the knotting. Set up the holding board thread with the clips: the color doesn't matter since this thread will be removed at the end. Install four 43 in. (110 cm) strands with soft overhand knots—these will be untied later. Make the overhand knots, leaving about 8 in. (20 cm) of cords above the holding cord; these will be used later to make a braid. On each side, add five 79 in. (200 cm) strands, fold them in the middle, and install with lark's head knots. (1)

**STEP 2** Tie the two central cords with a double half hitch knot and use these same two strands as holding cords to make two diagonal lines going from the center to both sides. Repeat the step to create a second line on each side. When you reach the ends of the second lines, don't forget to also tie the holding cords used to make the first lines. (2, 3, 4, 5)

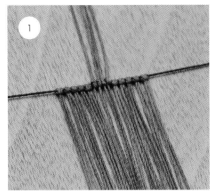

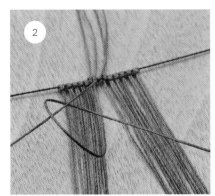

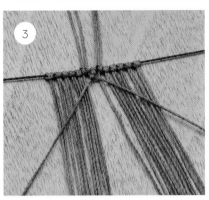

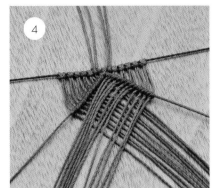

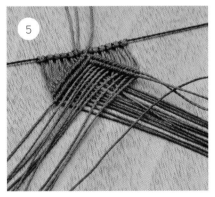

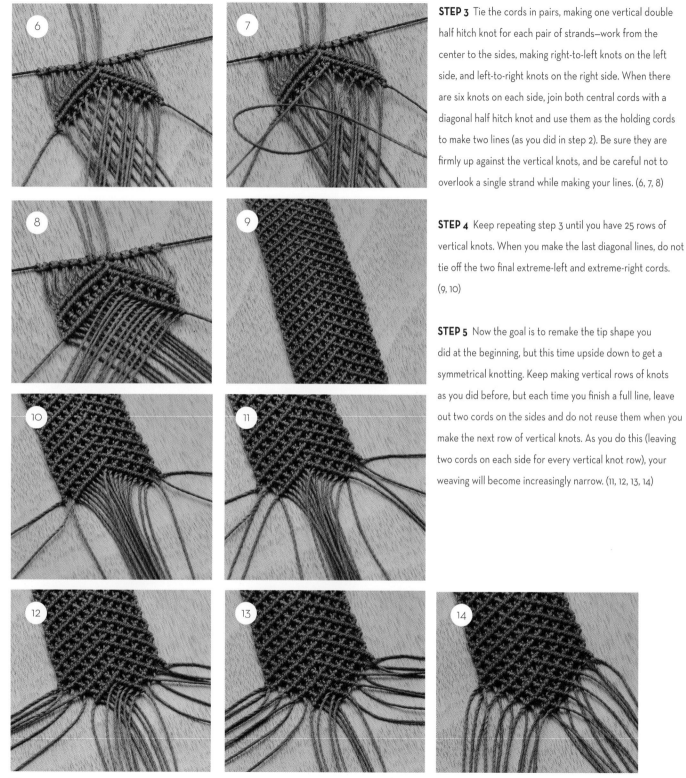

**STEP 3** Tie the cords in pairs, making one vertical double half hitch knot for each pair of strands—work from the center to the sides, making right-to-left knots on the left side, and left-to-right knots on the right side. When there are six knots on each side, join both central cords with a diagonal half hitch knot and use them as the holding cords to make two lines (as you did in step 2). Be sure they are firmly up against the vertical knots, and be careful not to overlook a single strand while making your lines. (6, 7, 8)

**STEP 4** Keep repeating step 3 until you have 25 rows of vertical knots. When you make the last diagonal lines, do not tie off the two final extreme-left and extreme-right cords. (9, 10)

**STEP 5** Now the goal is to remake the tip shape you did at the beginning, but this time upside down to get a symmetrical knotting. Keep making vertical rows of knots as you did before, but each time you finish a full line, leave out two cords on the sides and do not reuse them when you make the next row of vertical knots. As you do this (leaving two cords on each side for every vertical knot row), your weaving will become increasingly narrow. (11, 12, 13, 14)

**STEP 6** When your last four vertical rows are complete, use the second-farthest-left and second-farthest-right strands as the holding cords. Knot each of the other strings (except the farthest left and right), making one line on each side, then join them in the middle. Don't forget a single strand, and make sure all the diagonal knots are tightly up against the vertical ones. Repeat this step to create a second line with the farthest-right and farthest-left strands. (15, 16)

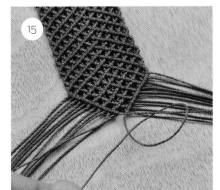
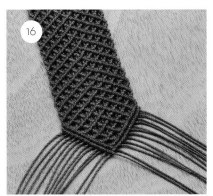

**STEP 7** Make another similar weaving, but instead of adding five 79 in. (200 cm) strands on each side in step 1, you need to install only three to make a thinner macramé knotting. You can use the same holding board thread. (17)

**STEP 8** Unclip your weavings, pull off the holding board thread, and clip the knotting back upside down. Untie the overhand knots and make a 7 in. (18 cm) simple braid or plait on each knotting. At the end, secure them with a big overhand knot. If you want, you can customize your tiara at this point by adding a bead. Finally, cut and melt all the remaining threads around your knotting. Keep the longest strands to use later to join the three different weavings together and to create the sliding knot. (18)

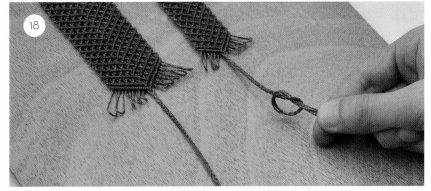

**Part 2: Decorative section**

**STEP 9** To make the strip of overlapping squares, start by securing the holding board thread horizontally across the board (you can use the same holding board cord as before). With lark's head knots, install all eight 90 in. (230 cm) strands, folding each in the middle. Separate into two equal groups of eight cords.

**STEP 10** With the left-side group, make a horizontal line with double half hitch knots, working from left to right to the center point. Repeat with the other group, this time making a line from right to left. Join the two holding cords together with a double half hitch knot, then clip them away at the top of the board. They are not used again in this first part of the pattern. (19, 20)

**STEP 11** Repeat step 10 seven more times. Don't forget to leave and clip out of the way both holding cords after the lines are joined in the middle. A triangle shape will start to form. Work until you have only two cords to tie together at the end. (21, 22)

**STEP 12** Separate the right and left strands into two groups, with the same number of strands on each side. With the upper thread as the holding cord, make one vertical line of horizontal double half hitch knots with each group. You can turn the board around if it makes things easier. (23, 24)

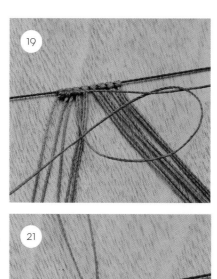
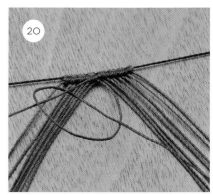
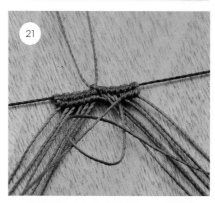
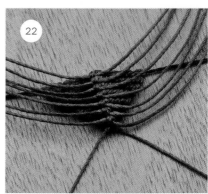
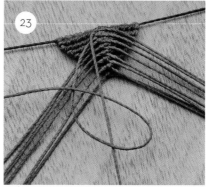
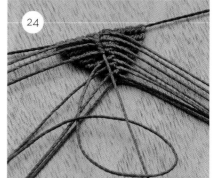

**STEP 13** Repeat step 12 six times on both sides, until another triangle shape appears. (25)

**STEP 14** Separate the strands again into two equal groups: use the farthest-left and farthest-right strands to make one horizontal line on each side. These will be joined in the middle. (26, 27, 28)

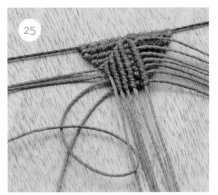

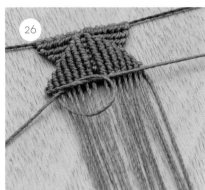

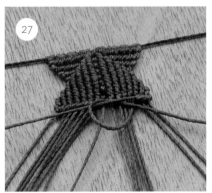

**STEP 15** The position of the strands should now be back as they were at the start. Keep repeating the steps until there are seven full overlapping squares, plus half of one that finishes with a last horizontal line. (29)

**STEP 16** Unclip and pull off the holding board thread. Cut and melt every remaining thread on both sides. Well done! Your three parts are now complete; you only have to join them together to enjoy your macramé tiara. (30)

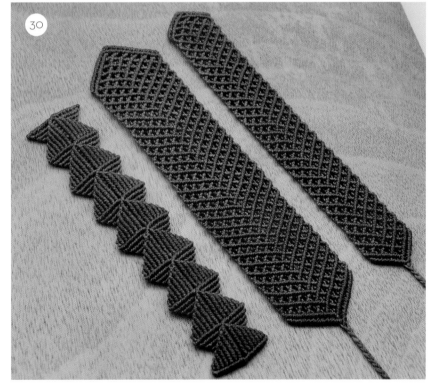

## Part 3: Finishing

**STEP 17** Start by joining both flat parts together. Place the thinner under the wider one, as shown in photo 31. With a strong needle and the already cut cords, pass the thread through both knottings, working from below and then from above. Finish with a tight overhand knot at the back. Do this on at least four points to secure them together firmly before cutting and melting. Do the same to add the strip of overlapping squares on the wide flat front. Adjust the position any way you like. I usually leave half of the flat part. (31, 32, 33)

**STEP 18** Use a length of cord at least 8 in. (20 cm) long to create the sliding knot. Prepare an overhand knot at its middle and pass both braids through before tying it. Make about 10 spiral square knots and finally cut the remaining strings on both sides of the sliding knot. Your tiara is now ready to wear. (34)

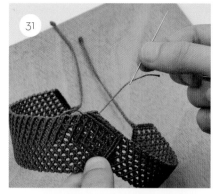

# Flower Barrette

Clip back your hair and keep up that carefree summer spirit all year round with this fashionable, lightweight floral barrette. It will surely bring you lots of attention and compliments! You can change its size by varying the number of flowers and the way you wear it. Try using an elastic hair holder instead of the barrette, or simply pin it on your dress or jacket and use it as a brooch.

**Knots used:**

Horizontal double half hitch knot, overhand knot, reverse lark's head knot, vertical double half hitch knot

**Macramé strands:**

All lengths of 1 mm waxed thread

**Big flower:**

8 x Dark purple, 8 in. (20 cm)

1 x Dark purple, 212 in. (540 cm)

8 x Camel orange, 20 in. (50 cm)

8 x Army green, 16 in. (40 cm)

8 x Ocher red, 12 in. (30 cm)

8 x Light green, 5 in. (12 cm)

**Small flowers (for two flowers):**

12 x Dark purple, 6 in. (15 cm)

2 x Dark purple, 118 in. (300 cm)

12 x Camel orange, 14 in. (35 cm)

12 x Army green, 10 in. (25 cm)

12 x Light green, 5 in. (12 cm)

4 x Camel orange, 6 in. (15 cm) to join the flowers

2 x Dark purple, 6 in. (15 cm) to add the barrette (optional)

**Materials:**

1 x 3 in. (8 cm) French-style barrette hair clip

Clips (optional)

Knotting board

Lighter and ruler

Multifunction glue (optional)

Needle and scissors

**Dimensions:**

This flower barrette is 6 in. (15 cm) long, but you can adjust the length depending on how you join the flowers at the end. It is 3 in. (8 cm) at its widest and 2 in. (5 cm) at the narrowest. An unusual element with this knotting is that you will not use clips to secure it while weaving. However, you can use them if it helps you make your knots, but since you have to work by continually turning the weaving, you will have to clip and unclip, over and over again.

**STEP 1** Each flower is made separately, so let's start with the big one. Place one 8 in. (20 cm) dark purple strand horizontally across the knotting board. Then install seven more strands on the horizontal strand, folding each in the center and placing them with reverse lark's head knots. Make sure they are positioned exactly at the middle of the holding strand. Turn your board and, using the holding strand as the knotting cord, tie a double half hitch knot: this will create a 16-rayed, sun-shape circle. (1, 2)

**STEP 2** Take the long 212 in. (540 cm) purple cord and prepare (i.e., form but don't secure) a simple overhand knot on one end, but don't tighten it. Pass any one of the rays through the prepared knot and tie it as closely as possible to the circle. Secure this long cord around the same ray with only one vertical half hitch knot loop. The result of the overhand knot plus the vertical loop should be the same as if you have made a vertical double half hitch knot. (3, 4)

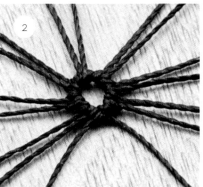

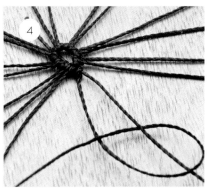

**STEP 3** Keep using the long strand as the knotting cord to make another vertical double half hitch knot around the next ray. Take one orange thread, fold it in half, then install it by making a reverse lark's head knot around the long purple thread, then push it tightly against the preceding vertical knot. (5, 6)

**STEP 4** As before, make one vertical double half hitch knot around the next two rays. Be careful not to skip a ray—an easy mistake to make at this stage of the knotting. Keep repeating the same color pattern by placing one orange thread, followed by two vertical double half hitch knots all the way around the circle. (7)

**STEP 5** After placing the last orange cord, go around a second time, still making vertical knots on the rays, but this time tie each orange thread with horizontal double half hitch knots around the long purple cord. On completing the circle and weaving in the last orange strand, knot only the next two rays, plus the next orange strand. (8, 9)

**STEP 6** Take one army green cord and attach it in exactly the same way as the previous orange ones—with a reverse lark's head knot pushed up tightly to the previous knot. Then knot the second orange strand with a horizontal half hitch knot. Go all the way around, installing every dark green cord between two orange cords. So I don't make mistakes, I keep repeating to myself at every step: *don't forget to keep knotting every ray with a vertical knot until the end of the weaving.* (10, 11, 12)

**STEP 7** Make a fourth round of knotting, using the same technique as you did for the second row—i.e., knotting every orange and army green cord with horizontal double half hitch knots. (13)

For the fifth round, place one red strand between each army green knot. (14, 15, 16)

For the sixth round, knot every cord. (17)

For the seventh, add one light green thread between each red strand. (18)

Finally, for the eighth round, knot every strand. (19)

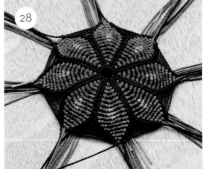

**STEP 8** Half of the petals are done, and no more thread needs to be added. Now the aim is to reduce the number of threads to give shape to the petals. To do so, knot a new row around the macramé circle as before, but omitting the first light green strands at each occurrence—leave them under the knotting. Knot only the second ones. Tie your knots firmly so they are tight up against the previous red knots. (20, 21)

**STEP 9** Make the 10th circle line, leaving out the second light green strands. The ray pairs will start to spread and a cord gap between each petal will appear—don't worry; this is what we want. As you knot, make sure the new ray knots are tight up against the orange knots. (22, 23)

**STEP 10** For the next two lines, leave out the first red strands and then, next time around, the second ones. Keep using this knotting technique until there is only one orange strand left to knot. As you work, the knotting will start to bulge and distort—this is to be expected—it will become flat again in the next step, when you cut the strands between each petal. (24, 25, 26, 27, 28)

**STEP 11** Weave a final round line by knotting only the ray lines with vertical half hitch knots. Finally, to create the ends of the petals, join the rays together by tying the cords coming out of the tips with a last double half hitch knot. Your macramé flower is complete! Carefully cut and melt all the strands between and under the petals to finish it off neatly. (29, 30, 31)

**STEP 12** For the smaller flowers the technique is exactly the same, except you use fewer strands. Use six 6 in. (15 cm) purple strands for the central circle. Add the long purple cord around one ray and start the lines by adding first the orange, then the army green, and finally the light green threads before leaving them out one by one until you have only one last orange left to knot. Finish your flowers by repeating step 11. (32, 33)

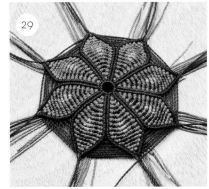

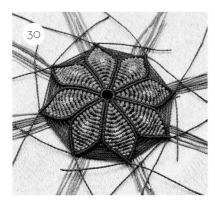

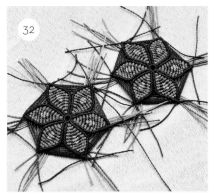

**Step 13** To join the flowers together, start with the small ones. Put one on top of the other, facing the same direction. With the needle, pass one 6 in. (15 cm) orange cord from underneath and then back from above—but do this through an orange knot so it won't be visible from the front. Join this cord together at the back and make a tight overhand knot. Do this on at least two points, then do the same again to secure the big flower. Make as many knots as you want to bind the flowers together, but keep free the place where you intend to attach your metal barrette. Cut and melt any remaining cords. (34, 35, 36)

**Attaching your Macramé**

To complete your macramé barrette, you have two options. If your metal clip has two holes (as in my example), you can use the same sewing technique as before—using a strand through the hole and the flower before making a big knot. If your clip has no hole, you can simply stick it by using a multifunction glue that can stick metal and textile together. (37, 38)

# CLUTCH BAG

Customize any kind of clutch bag with a personal touch and blast of color with this stylish macramé knotting. Use it for an evening bag to accessorize a special outfit, or for a makeup bag, or even a very individual pencil case—in fact, any useful small bag.

**Knots used:**

Horizontal diagonal half hitch knot, lark's head knot, overhand knot, vertical double half hitch knot

**Macramé strands:**

All lengths of 1 mm waxed thread

3 x Coral pink, 49 in. (125 cm)

3 x Dark brown, 49 in. (125 cm)

8 x Dark brown, 142 in. (360 cm)

8 x Dark brown, 20 in. (50 cm)

3 x Lavender, 49 in. (125 cm)

3 x Ocher red, 49 in. (125 cm)

3 x Peach, 49 in. (125 cm)

3 x Purple, 49 in. (125 cm)

3 x Straw, 49 in. (125 cm)

3 x White, 49 in. (125 cm)

1 holding board strand, the width of the board

**Materials:**

1 clutch bag

Knotting board and clips

Ruler and lighter

Scissors

Textile glue

**Dimensions:**

For this project I have used a 10 x 7.5 in. (25 x 19 cm) clutch bag. However, if your bag is a different size, you can adjust it: for every 4 in. (10 cm), allow about 20 in. (50 cm) of threads for the very small squares, and about 65 in. (165 cm) of threads to make 4 in. (10 cm) of the overlapping big squares.

**STEP 1** Begin by working on the very small squares. Clip the holding strand horizontally across the board—the color does not matter since it is pulled off when the weaving is complete. Using simple overhand knots, tie one purple thread. To the right, install three dark brown, then three peach, three ocher red, and two lavender strands. To the left of the purple strand, place one lavender, then three straw, three coral pink, three white, and two purple strands. (1)

**STEP 2** With the two central purple and lavender cords, tie a double half hitch knot. Use these two same strands as holding cords to make one diagonal line on each side, working from the center to both sides. (2, 3, 4)

**STEP 3** Using the first straw-colored thread as the holding cord, tie every dark brown with horizontal double half hitch knots. Repeat with the second and third straw threads to create a small dark brown square.

The straw threads now become the knotting threads to make the second square. Take the first straw cord (the one coming out from the first brown line) and tie it around each peach strand, using vertical double half hitch knots. Repeat with the second and third straw threads to complete the second square. (5, 6, 7, 8, 9, 10—see overleaf)

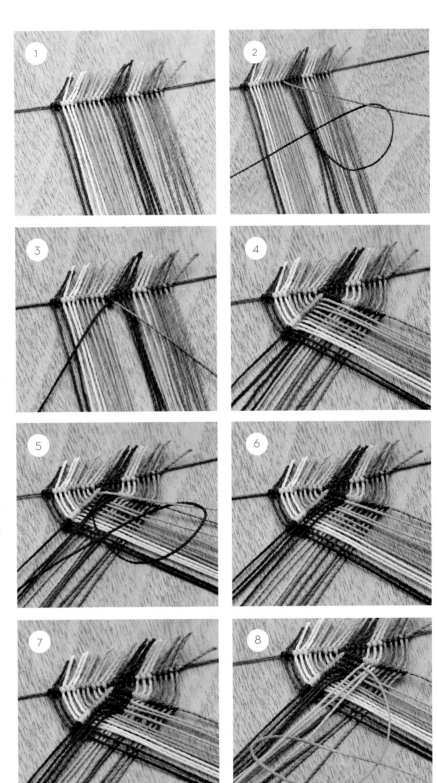

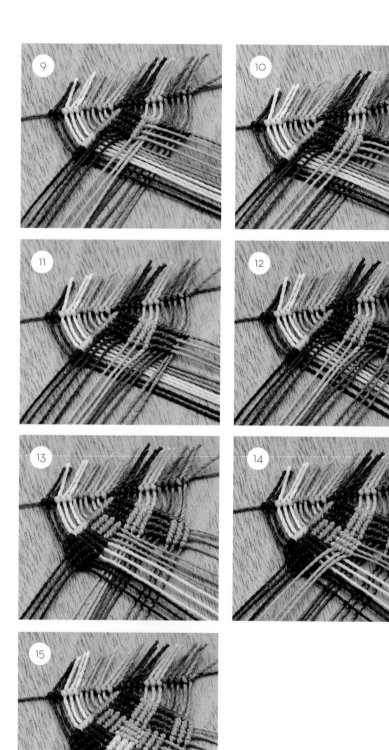

**STEP 4** Keep working on the same side and make a third ocher red square, using the straw-colored strands as the holding cords (as before with the brown). Complete the right-side row of squares the same way with a second straw square, but do not forget to also use the lavender strand coming out from the line you made in step 2. (11, 12)

**STEP 5** Knot three squares on the left side: one coral pink square with the dark brown strands as holding cords, one dark brown square using the white strands as holding cords and vertical double half hitch knots, and finally, a purple square with the brown holding cords. (13)

**STEP 6** Make a peach square between the coral pink and the straw squares. Use the coral pink strands as holding cords and tie each peach strand around them. Then create a white square between the peach and the dark brown, by knotting each white around every peach strand. Between the peach and the ocher red squares, make another square by tying each coral pink thread around every ocher red strand. Finish this step by doing an ocher red square between the white and coral pink squares. (14, 15)

**STEP 7** Still using the same technique, work on the left side to knot a peach square between the purple and the white one. Then knot a purple square between the peach and the central ocher red square. Moving to the right side, knot a lavender square between the straw and the coral pink squares, then a white square between the lavender and the ocher red. Finish this step by knotting a lavender square between the purple and the white squares. (16, 17)

**STEP 8** Keep repeating the pattern, but alternating the square colors and making sure that every square is perpendicular to the previous one. When you make the farthest-right and farthest-left squares, be particularly careful to make them perpendicular to the previous squares. You must also adjust the tightness of your knots to leave small gaps of cord—check your knotting against the photos. (18, 19)

**STEP 9** To finish the weaving and make it symmetrical, you have to re-create the triangular shape made at the start. If you have kept knotting the pattern by making three squares on the right and then three squares on the left, with a finishing central square, the triangular end will have appeared. However, if you made the squares randomly this won't have happened. So, to re-create the triangular end, you have to make a row of four horizontal squares, then a row of three squares, followed by a row of two squares, and finally a last central square. (20, 21, 22, 23)

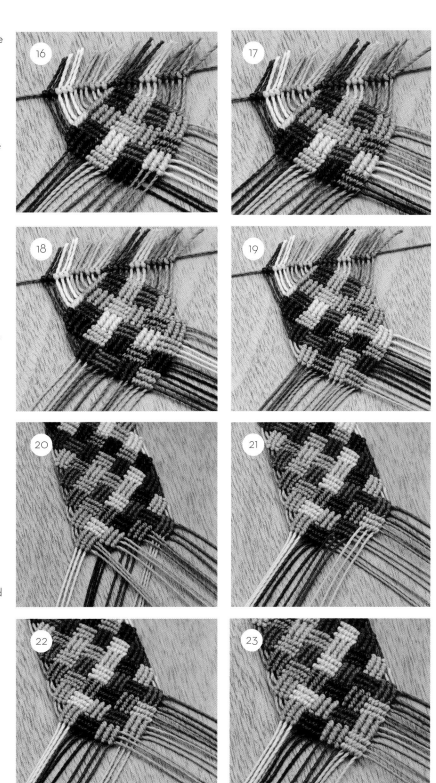

**STEP 10** Complete your triangular shape by using the farthest-left and farthest-right cords. Make one line on each side, going from the sides to the center, and join both cords in the middle. Pull off the holding board thread. Cut and melt every remaining strand left jutting out on both sides. (24, 25, 26)

**STEP 11** Now it's time for the overlapping big squares. Refer back to the Tiara project (see page 94) and follow steps 9 through 16. You can use the same holding board thread as before, but this time use the 142 in. (360 cm) dark brown strands. The only difference between both projects is that here you have to knot 13 full squares instead of seven. (27, 28, 29)

**STEP 12** Make the third and last section by repeating the previous step, but make only one full square with the 20 in. (50 cm) dark brown strands. Be careful—you have to leave out the holding cords under the weaving instead of above when you knot the second half of the full square. This way the cutting and melting can be done underneath the knotting for a neater finish. (30, 31)

### Attaching your Macramé

Position the first section of small squares on your bag. Then evenly apply the special fabric glue across the underside of the macramé and where it's needed on the bag. Let the glue dry for a couple of minutes, then place the two together. Repeat the process with the second and third weavings to finish your customed clutch bag. Alternatively, if your bag is made of fabric you can sew the macramé weavings into position. (32)

32

# Mandala Bag

This personalized summer straw bag is ideal to take to the beach, bursting with all your essentials, or to carry around at a music festival, filled with everything you need. It is inspired by the colorful style of the 1970s but is modernized with a boho look. The best part is that no one else will have a bag the same as yours!

**Knots used:**

Diagonal double half hitch knot, lark's head knot, overhand knot, vertical double half hitch knot

**Macramé strands:**

All lengths of 1 mm waxed thread

(Enough for one mandala, so multiply the number of strands according to how many mandalas you want to make)

6 x Straw, 16 in. (40 cm)

6 x Straw, 8 in. (20 cm)

6 x Fuchsia pink, 16 in. (20 cm)

6 x Royal blue, 16 in .(30 cm)

6 x Purple, 16 in. (30 cm)

12 x Turquoise, 8 in. (20 cm)

**Materials:**

One round straw bag 16 x 16 in. (40 x 40 cm)

Clips and lighter (optional)

Knotting board

Ruler

Scissors

Textile glue

**Dimensions:**

The size of the mandala is about 2.5 in. (6 cm), depending on how tightly you tie your knots. The main difficulty here is that you do not use clips to secure your weaving. Actually, you could use them if you find it easier, but you will have to clip, unclip, and clip again numerous times as you knot all around the mandala. Uniquely, with this project, you macramé on its underside and see the final result only when you flip it over at the end. You can, of course, use a smaller or bigger bag, depending on your patience!

**STEP 1** Place one 16 in. (40 cm) straw strand across your board, without clipping it. Install five more strands, folding them in the middle and using lark's head knots. Ensure they are placed exactly at the center of the holding strand. And finally, use this same holding cord as the knotting cord to do a double half hitch knot. It will create a 12-rayed, sun-shaped circle. (1, 2)

**STEP 2** Join the rays in pairs to get a six-rayed, sun-shaped circle. Add one fuchsia strand on each pair of rays, using a simple overhand knot in the middle. Make this knot in reverse so that the loop of the knot is visible. Repeat the process all around the circle, using the royal blue and then purple strands. (3, 4)

**STEP 3** Tie each pair of straw strands together with a double half hitch knot to secure the previous cords you've already installed. Keep working with the rays one at a time. Choose any ray and use the straw-colored threads as holding cords. Tie the fuchsia pink cords with a diagonal double half hitch knot on each side. Be sure the pink cords pass underneath the blue and purple ones, and do not tie them too hard—make sure you keep the gap between the first overhand knot and this knot. Repeat this step on each ray all around the circle. (5, 6)

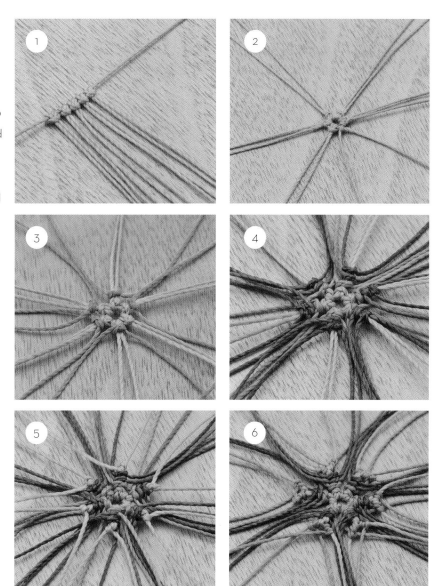

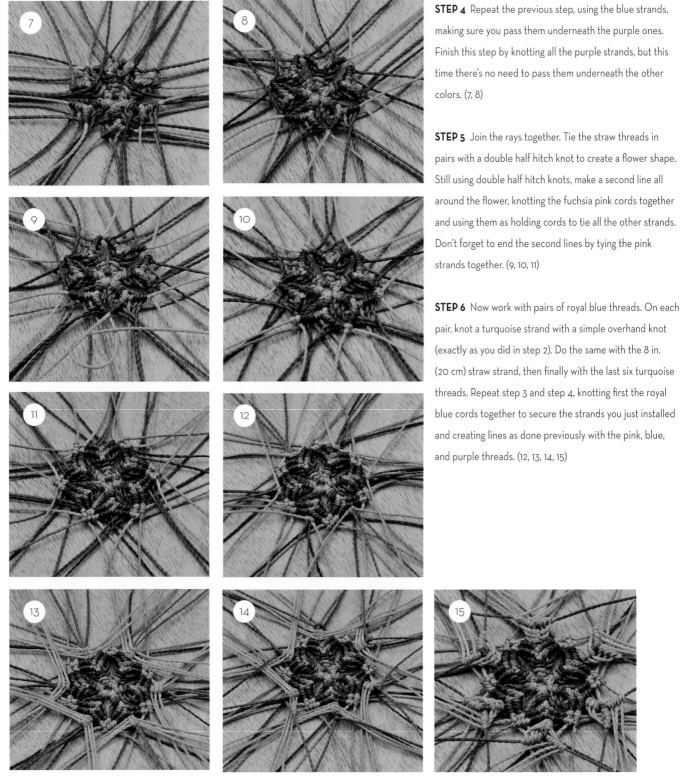

**STEP 4** Repeat the previous step, using the blue strands, making sure you pass them underneath the purple ones. Finish this step by knotting all the purple strands, but this time there's no need to pass them underneath the other colors. (7, 8)

**STEP 5** Join the rays together. Tie the straw threads in pairs with a double half hitch knot to create a flower shape. Still using double half hitch knots, make a second line all around the flower, knotting the fuchsia pink cords together and using them as holding cords to tie all the other strands. Don't forget to end the second lines by tying the pink strands together. (9, 10, 11)

**STEP 6** Now work with pairs of royal blue threads. On each pair, knot a turquoise strand with a simple overhand knot (exactly as you did in step 2). Do the same with the 8 in. (20 cm) straw strand, then finally with the last six turquoise threads. Repeat step 3 and step 4, knotting first the royal blue cords together to secure the strands you just installed and creating lines as done previously with the pink, blue, and purple threads. (12, 13, 14, 15)

**STEP 7** Keep working with the turquoise and straw threads. Create a small second line, starting with knotting both central turquoise strands together and using these threads as the holding cords. Do the same with the straw strands to create a third, even smaller, line. Finally, knot together the central turquoise strands. Repeat this step all around your mandala. (16)

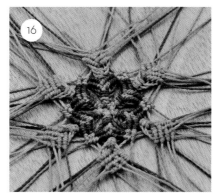

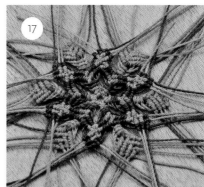

**STEP 8** Move to work with the pink and purple threads. Choose any of the six sections and use the pink threads as holding cords to knot the straw and purples threads on each side. Make a second small line on both sides by knotting both central straw strands and the purple strands. Finish this step by tying the central purple strands together, then repeat all around the knotting. (17)

**STEP 9** To complete the mandala, join every part together with vertical double half hitch knots, using the royal blue strands as knotting cords to create a final line (above the purple line). Do not forget to join the royal blue strands together when they meet. (18)

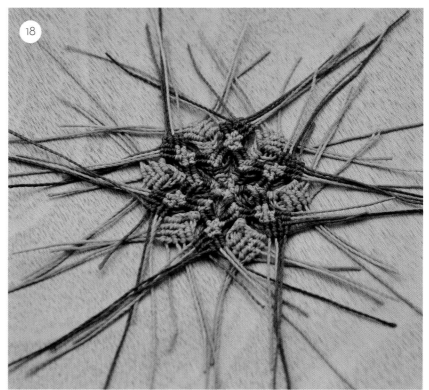

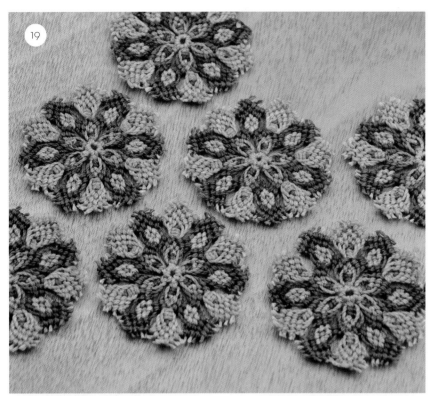

**STEP 10** Finish the weaving by cutting the surplus strands. I cut mine by leaving a tiny bit of cord, about 2 mm. If you do this, be sure your last knots are well tightened so they do not reopen. You can also cut them by leaving a millimeter, and carefully burn/melt the ends. This way the knots will be secure. Turn your macramé over to see what you've made. (19, 20)

**Attaching your Macramé**

Knot as many mandalas as necessary to cover the face side of your round bag. Plan out how you want to place the mandalas, then sew them (or glue them) one by one, starting from the center. (21, 22)

# TRIBAL DRAWING DENIM JACKET BACK

This striking and colorful macramé design will make your classic denim jacket an enviable statement piece and uniquely your own.

**Knots used:**

Lark's head knot, horizontal double half hitch knot, overhand knot, vertical double half hitch knot.

**Macramé strands:**

All lengths of 1 mm waxed thread

**Tribal Drawing central panel:**

1 holding board strand the width of the board

8 x Dark purple, 71 in. (180 cm)

8 x Lime green, 51 in. (130 cm)

8 x Army green, 90 in. (230 cm)

4 x Straw, 110 in. (280 cm)

2 x Orange, 63 in. (160 cm)

2 x Dark red, 110 in. (280 cm)

**Tribal Drawing side panels (two strips):**

1 holding board strand the width of the board

8 x Straw, 55 in. (140 cm)

4 x White, 32 in. (80 cm)

4 x Dark purple, 102 in. (260 cm)

4 x Dark purple, 67 in. (170 cm)

4 x Army green, 110 in. (280 cm)

4 x Dark red, 39 in. (100 cm)

4 x Orange, 83 in. (210 cm)

4 x Lime green, 110 in. (280 cm)

**Monochrome strips (for eight strips):**

1 holding board strand the width of the board

4 x Ocher red, 181 in. (460 cm)

2 x Ocher red, 73 in. (185 cm)

4 x Straw, 181 in. (460 cm)

2 x Straw, 73 in. (185 cm)

4 x Dark red, 181 in. (460 cm)

2 x Dark red, 73 in. (185 cm)

4 x Light brown, 181 in. (460 cm)

2 x Light brown, 73 in. (185 cm)

**Materials:**

One denim jacket

Needle and nylon sewing cord

Knotting board and clips

Ruler and lighter

6 x snap fasteners

Scissors

**Dimensions:**

The width of this macramé panel is 7 in. (18 cm) by approximately 13 in. (33 cm) long. If you need to modify the width, it's easy—you just have to add or remove plain monochrome strips—each thin strip measures 3/8 in. (0.9 cm). To adjust the length of your strips and avoid wasting your cord unnecessarily, divide the strand length by 13 if using inches and 33 if centimeters, then multiply the result by the number of inches or centimeters desired.

## Using the Grid

To create this macramé weaving, you first need to understand how to read this pattern illustration and how to use it while weaving. The main difference with this project is that you weave the backside —the underside—and see the final result only when you turn it over at the end. It's easier to make the knots this way!

Before you start, I want to give you some advice to make things easier when you start this knotting.

The horizontal numbers are here to help you install the strands onto your holding board strand.

Always work row by row (vertical numbers); do not try to make a knot and then the one below it. Keep following the row order from left to right (or from right to left); it does not matter so long as you

make all the knots of one row before starting the next one.
At the end of the row, you can work the next row by working back in the other direction, or return to the beginning point and continue working in the same direction as the first row. It's up to you, but be consistent for even knotting.

Carefully follow the vertical numbers; you'll see that on one line out of two you have to leave one cord on each side (the tips without circles on the sides)—these cords are not used to make this row. But don't forget to take them back in to knot the next row!

In the diagram, the color of the circles represents the knotting cord. It means that when you've made your knot, this is the color you should see, the holding thread being hidden inside the knot.

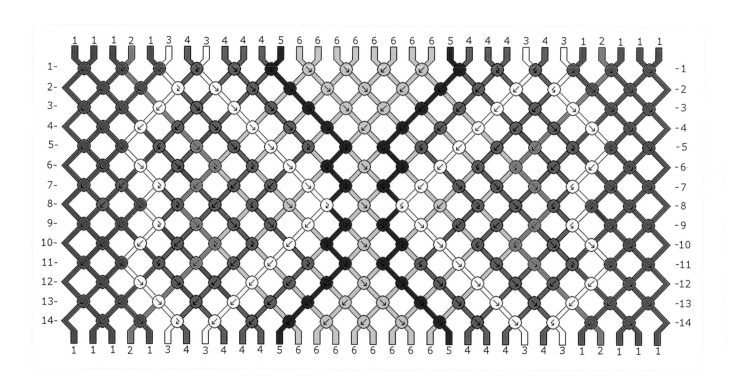

**Key**

The arrow describes the direction of the knots:

Both first knots are standard double half hitch knots. When the arrow is pointing right, the left strand is the knotting one, and vice versa when the arrow is pointing left.

When the arrow comes from the right but then points back to the right, it means that the knotting cord is the right one and that you have to make a first normal loop as a simple double half hitch knot, then change hands so that the second loop comes back on the right side. When the arrow comes from left and goes back to the left, reverse these directions.

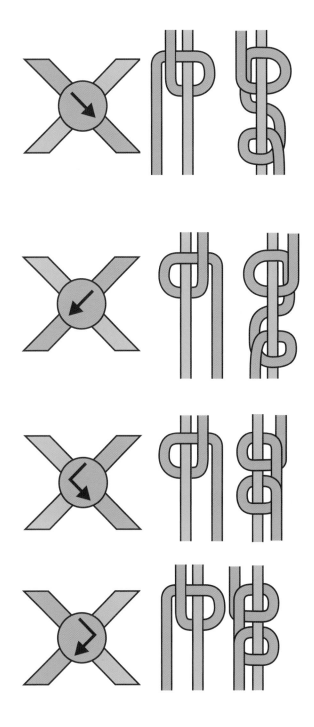

**Tribal Drawing, central panel**

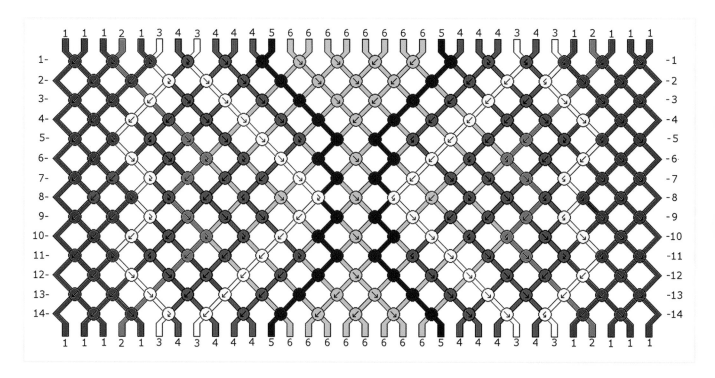

**STEP 1** Start by clipping your holding board strand to the board. Following the horizontal numbers, use simple overhand knots to place every strand in the color order shown in the diagram. (1)

**STEP 2** Following the diagram, make the knots row by row until row 14. This completes one cycle of the pattern and returns the cords to the same order as at the beginning. Start again at the first row and repeat the 14-row cycle. For this project, I made a total of 14 cycles to get the length needed. (2, 3)

**STEP 3** To finish this section of the tribal strip and secure the last row of knots, turn your weaving over to work on its back. Make a line with horizontal double half hitch knots, using the first right and first left threads as the holding cords, before joining them when they meet in the middle. (4)

**STEP 4** Unclip and cut your holding board thread, leaving a couple of millimeters of the cords. Carefully melt the ends to be sure that the sides knots will not open. Then cut and melt all the other remaining strands on both edges of your strip. (5, 6)

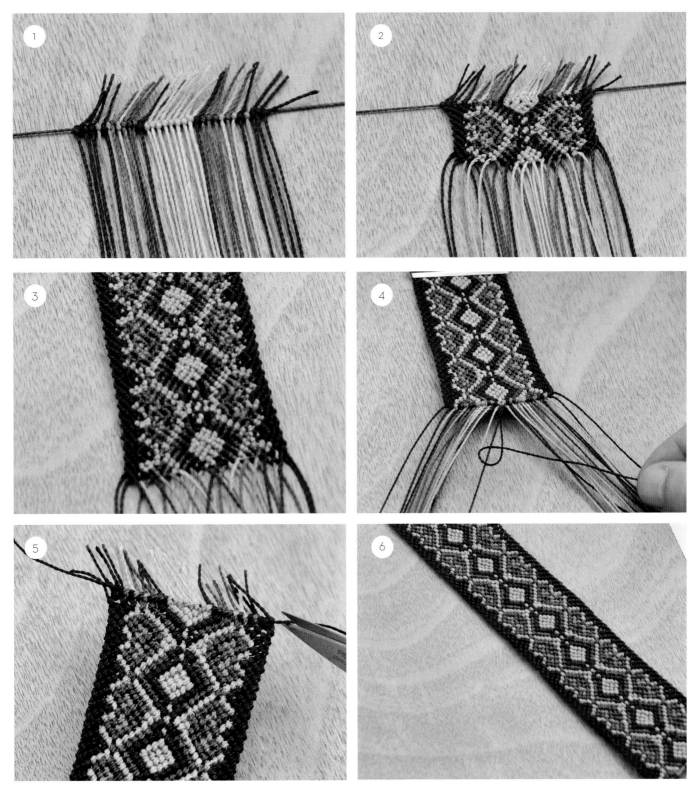

**Tribal Drawing, side panel**

**STEP 5** This pattern is simpler than the central piece, so it should be much easier now! Clip your holding board strand and, with simple overhand knots, install every strand in the order shown in the diagram above. Pay attention here! Install the longer dark purple strands on the edge of either side, and the shorter ones between the straw strands in the center. (7)

**STEP 6** As before for the central panel, make your macramé knots row by row while following the diagram pattern. When you reach the 14th row, repeat the pattern in cycles until you have a matching length with the central panel. (8, 9)

**STEP 7** As before with the central panel in step 3, turn your weaving over and knot a last horizontal line to secure the last row. (10)

**STEP 8** Make one more macramé strip to get two of them. You can use the same holding board thread without removing the first strip you made, but be very careful not to pull off the thread! It can be useful as a color guide for the second strip.

**STEP 9** Unclip and cut your holding board cord, leaving a couple of millimeters of cords on each side of both weavings. Melt them carefully to be sure the sides knots will not open. Then cut and melt all the other remaining strands on both ends of your strips.

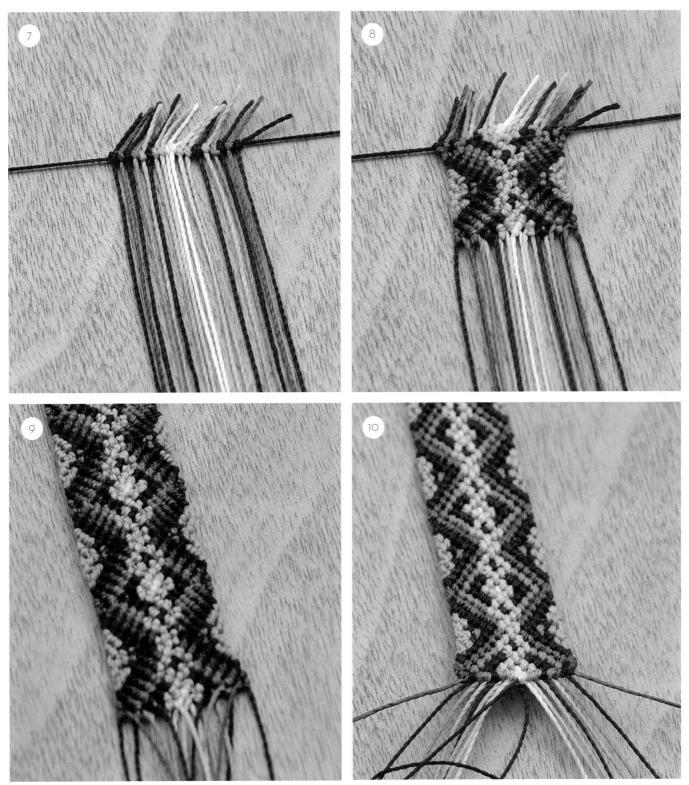

**Monochrome strip sections**

**STEP 10** To create one monochrome strip, you need two 181 in. (460 cm) strands, plus one 73 in. (185 cm) strand. Choose a color for the first strip. Clip your holding board thread in place—the color doesn't matter since it is pulled off at the end. Install the 73 in. (185 cm) strand with a loose overhand knot—since you will undo it later. Then fold the two 181 in. (460 cm) lengths exactly in the middle and install them next to each other, using lark's head knots.

**STEP 11** The 73 in. (185 cm) thread will ALWAYS be the holding cord throughout—this way it will be hidden inside the knots. The four other strands are the knotting ones. Take the holding cord and knot every other cord with horizontal double half hitch knots to create a line. This line has to be tightly up against the holding board cord. (11, 12)

**STEP 12** When you reach the end of the line after knotting your four cords, keep using the same holding cord, only changing hands and knotting back the same strands in reverse order to create a second line. Again, make sure it is tightly up against the previous row of knots. (13, 14)

**STEP 13** Repeat the knots from one side to another until your strip is complete. (15)

**STEP 14** Make seven more strips, by repeating steps 10–13. On finishing, pull off the holding board thread and undo the overhand knot. Cut and neatly melt every leftover end so the knots do not reopen. (16)

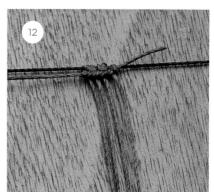
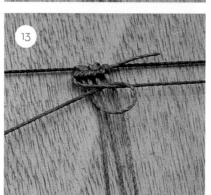
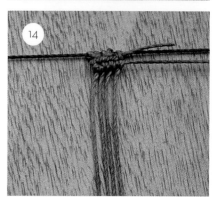
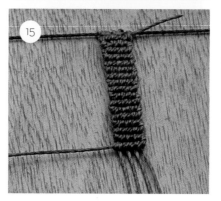
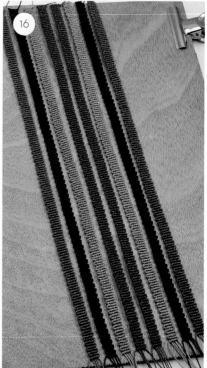

**Sewing the panels together**

**STEP 15** I like to work with the weavings upside down because I like the look of the back of the knotting, but you can, of course, choose whichever side you prefer. Using transparent nylon sewing cord (for invisibility), join the pieces together with a long stitched seam. Then add at least six half snap fasteners to the outer edges, three on each side. (17)

**Attaching your Macramé**

Finish your creation by sewing on the other halves of the snaps to the back of your jacket—make sure they are exactly aligned with the ones on your macramé panel. (18)

17

18

Gwenaël Petiot was born in 1983 and raised in Aix-en-Provence, France. At age 15 he moved to Canada to play ice hockey, then in 2001 he returned home to France to study lighting direction at audiovisual school. After working as an assistant lighting director in the television industry for a period, he quit his job in 2007 and traveled around South America. There Gwenaël discovered the craft that would become his passion—macramé. Needing to fund his adventures, he asked some Peruvian and Argentinian friends to teach him the secrets of macramé. He began by selling his creations on the street and earned enough money to travel for the next four years, visiting ten different countries, including Bolivia, Brazil, Ecuador, and Colombia.

Gwenaël returned to France in 2011, determined to use his newfound skills to earn a freewheeling living selling macramé jewelry. He went from selling his wares at craft markets around France to debuting his designs on the catwalk as part of the Spring 2012 haute couture collection with French designer Anne Valérie Hash, the inspiration for this book. From time to time his remarkable creations can be seen adorning the famous Cirque du Soleil artistes.

He now lives in Paris and has never stopped enjoying the satisfaction of creating something amazing with knots and string.